P9-EDQ-070

Living In The World As If It Were Home

Living In The World As If It Were Home

Essays

Tim Lilburn

CORMORANT BOOKS

The publisher gratefully acknowledges the support of
the Canada Council for the Arts and the Ontario Arts
Council for its publishing program. We acknowledge
the financial support of the Government of Canada
through the Book Publishing Industry Development
Program (BPIDP) for our publishing activities.

Printed and bound in Canada.

Canadian Cataloguing in Publication Data
Lilburn, Tim, 1950-
Living in the world as if it were home
Essays.
ISBN 1-896951-14-7
1. Philosophy of nature. I. Title.
PS8573.I427L59 1999   C814'.54   C99-900063-2
PR9199.3.L514L59 1999

CORMORANT BOOKS INC.
RR 1, Dunvegan, Ontario K0C 1J0

To my mother, Winnifred Lilburn,
and in memory of my father, Walter Lilburn

The conviction which had come to me was that when one hungers for bread, one does not receive stones. . . . Just as I was certain that desire has in itself an efficacy in the realm of spiritual goodness, whatever its form, I thought it was also possible that it might not be effective in any other realm.

—Simone Weil, letter

Contents

FOREWORD

The first essay I read by Tim Lilburn was "How To Be Here?" I remember being struck by the sheer physicality of the prose. Sentences crackled and lunged; the thinking seemed both gnarled and acrobatic. All Lilburn's meditations have that animal gusto, even at their most formidably intellectual. I suspect the book in which they've been gathered will stand as a minor classic.

What kind of book is it? One of the pleasures of *Living In The World As If It Were Home* is that there's no simple answer. The essays defy existing categories, create a category of their own. Some readers will know instinctively what they're up to, just as some will find them permanently opaque. But there will also be readers who recognize the experience the essays explore, yet find themselves puzzled by the way they move. For Lilburn is pursuing at least four missions here, and he can shift from one to another in the blink of an eye. It might be useful to examine what holds them together.

The book's first mission is to look at creatures and things: simply to *look* at them. Lilburn was born in Regina, and most of his meditations burrow into parts of Saskatchewan which have become places of the heart for him. But he isn't searching for uplifting scenery, or dramatic vignettes. He just walks out in the ordinary scrubland he loves, and, with an almost unnerving concentration of desire, he looks at things. Whatever else he explores begins in this attention to the natural word.

One context for the essays, then, is the tradition of nature writing — even though Lilburn isn't steeped in the genre himself. He hasn't read Thoreau, Dillard, Lopez; he discovered John Muir and John Burroughs only a few years ago. But no matter. These are love letters to a river, two deer, a particular stretch of fescue grass, all seen with a clear yet exuberant eye.

IV

Another context for the essays is the contemplative tradition. Here it takes a little longer to get Lilburn's mission into focus.

When the man and the deer stand watching each other in "How to Be Here?", the man undergoes a double movement of feeling. One is awe, as he glimpses the creatures' way of being themselves. The other is mortification, as he realizes he will never penetrate their nature. Every attempt reduces them to abstract concepts, or sentimental symbols; meanwhile, "the deer show out from around the word 'deer' and they have no name". All his lofty thoughts and feelings have been strategies of possession, and futile ones at that. This double movement — of awe, and abashment — is the essays' centre of gravity. Lilburn hurls himself into it again and again, till the bare act of looking becomes a form of spiritual discipline.

This is not an idle claim, but to understand it we need some background. Lilburn was raised in the United Church, which was scarcely a hotbed of contemplative lore. (He grew up in a rough neighbourhood where his father was a mailman, and his mother worked in a dress store. His main after-school interests seem to have been hockey and fighting.) At twenty-one he became a Roman

Catholic; after a stint of teaching in Nigeria, and another of construction work, he joined the Jesuits. He began his training with the "long retreat" in which the novice retraces the spiritual exercises of St. Ignatius. And for nine years he alternated between periods of study and teaching. But in 1987, at thirty-seven, he left the order. There was no crisis of faith involved, though the change wasn't easy. He had simply recognized that he was in the wrong place. For the next three years he worked as a farm labourer.

One thing he came away with was the habit of daily meditation. And the contemplative tradition he felt at home in was the "negative way". This has not been the primary path in Western spirituality; it can be pursued only by men and women who find themselves drawn to it with no choice. In its classic form, which emerged in the monastic era, the apprentice's itch to possess things was progressively chastened. First he had to give up attachment to things of the world: money, sensual pleasures, security. Then his spiritual attachments were loosened; the sweetness of meditation, religious consolations, the knowledge of God's reality — all grew arid. His desire did not diminish, but the impulse to own or control what he desired was systematically frustrated. Even a conscious understanding of what was happening to him was withheld. Over months and years he was being scoured and infused by the Godhead, which had been the initiator all along. Seasoned contemplatives described this process as a "dazzling dark".

Lilburn discovered *The Cloud of Unknowing* when he was twenty, and that down-to-earth manual of negative devotion gave him his first sense of spiritual home. As he told me recently, "I saw that your engagement with the world could be thoughtful, erotic, athletic, without leaving the West." Soon he was soaking up other masters in the tradition; his favourites were some of the desert monks and early church fathers, whom he treats as familiar guides and companions.

It would be redundant to say more about the negative way itself here, since the essays explore it with such first-hand verve. But there are several things to notice in Lilburn's account. One is his language. There are almost no modern terms for the experience of naughting, so it was natural to adopt the categories of his mentors. Most readers will find them foreign, however, and Lilburn has come to dispense with more and more of the older terms. But he relies on a few of them still, like "penthos" and "apophasis". A reader who is prepared to absorb these terms — which are glossed at the end of the book — will soon find their strangeness diminishing.

A more startling aspect of Lilburn's account is that he relocates the basic discipline, of waiting in hunger and awe without expecting any spiritual candy. In monastic tradition, this reflex was trained during private prayer. Lilburn's practice has a different setting, though its dynamics are the same. As he observes rather cryptically in the Preface, he is "not interested in theology but in desire".

What does the shift entail? For many traditional contemplatives, nature was sinful, fallen, a place of temptation; relinquishing the itch to own things meant turning their backs on the world. But for Lilburn such a stance can easily become neurotic, even blasphemous. He urges instead that living in the natural world with "courtesy" can be a valid form of negative devotion. And when he parses the dynamics of looking with such drunken austerity, such poverty-stricken largesse, this is what he is pressing to show us. The bare act of waiting on a bird, a deer, a clump of wolf willow can instigate the chastening of possessive desire. "Contemplation of nature," he says, "like contemplation of God in negative theology, is a knowing which is an unknowing." And he continues,

> The knowing of discrete things, these sandhills, the
> rose hollows, chokecherry tufts dark in snow, the
> deer, is a not-knowing of them, a humbling of the
> mind's workaday craving for fixity, certitude.

This is a radical proposal, clearly anchored in personal
experience. It has nothing to do with the cult of romantic
Nature, where humans forage for exquisite sensations in
the wild. Nor is it merely a displaced version of monastic
contemplation. I take it to be an independent
contemporary expression of the negative way, with its
own strengths and pitfalls. I don't know any other modern
writer on spiritual practice who explores this path so
thoroughly, so unsparingly even.

When Lilburn looks at the deer, then, he wants to see
nothing but the deer. He isn't trying to press through to
some encounter with Deerness, or the Ineffable. Yet that
"nothing but" re-embodies a rich and rigorous devotional
tradition, which is called to a place of bare rapture.

For Lilburn, marvelling at natural things is both a gesture
of instinctive delight and a spiritual discipline. And it's
something else as well: a dislocation into poetry. This is
the book's third mission. It's clear that Lilburn has been
chosen by words; his muscular, radiant poems are
testimony to that. Hence the meditations of *Living In The
World As If It Were Home* stand as essays in poetics, even
when they don't mention the subject directly. The kind of
poetry they illuminate is the kind Tim Lilburn writes.

How can words ring true, when they say at once too
much and too little about what they address? About a
poplar, say, sheathed in morning ice? As always, Lilburn
starts with the experience of looking. And he identifies

the double movement we traced above as the life pulse of the poem. First he larrups ahead in a riot of naming — an erotic homage to the poplar, which can become jauntily absurd in its overabundance. Then he recoils into a tongue-tied abashment, as it becomes clear how little the words have to do with the tree's reality. "Language asserts and cancels itself, names the world then erases the names." And then the impulse to praise starts up again, in a fresh bout of naming. A reader who doesn't have one of

VIII Lilburn's collection on hand *(Moosewood Sandhills,* say, or *To the River)* can track these stages of verbal desire in the essays themselves.

More bio.

Lilburn now teaches philosophy and writing in a Catholic college, and that points to the final mission the essays pursue. From time to time they sift through philosophy, cosmology, theology, taking the experience of contemplating creatures and things as a kind of tuning fork. Which rational accounts of the world ring true, in light of that experience? Which seem inadequate or false?

For a reader who doesn't share Lilburn's background (such as myself), these pages are likely to prove the toughest sledding in the book. That's because most of the thinkers he considers come from the early centuries of Christianity, or the scholastic period. Certainly he re-animates many of the debates he discusses. And he keeps shifting back to the wilderness as a point of grounding. Nonetheless, it can be exhausting for a reader to absorb so much intellectual history.

Yet it pleases me somehow that Lilburn is so uncompromising. These were the modes of thought of his mentors, and he's not going to cut corners. And not only that: just when I'm ready to jump up and down on his head, urge him to stop *thinking* so much, I recognize what I take to be the larger point of these philosophic excursions.

In his argument with Augustine, we see Lilburn resisting a form of reason which brushes too quickly past the world's odd particularity, treats it as a tidy, expoundable allegory of the divine mind. By the same token, his quarrel with Descartes is a refusal of any thinking that would shrink the inscrutable world to mere "dimension and movement", which it can analyze from a safe distance. But there have been thinkers who refused to anaesthetize the world by declaring it rationally soluble. And in his celebration of Duns Scotus, for instance, we see him championing a cast of mind which respects the uniqueness of each thing. Thus he can write,

> How dare you assert the identity of a thing with something else when your gaze tells you that it is beyond all naming? Reverent attention reveals a thing's indifferent oddness before which you feel small.

Such particularity may be a scandal to reason — but it is precisely this scandal that can bring reason to recognize its poverty, and perhaps begin to love. Thus the philosophical mission of the essays traces the same dynamic as the other three, in fact coincides with them.

Poet, contemplative, thinker, hot-blooded lover of trees and rivers: is there anyone else like Lilburn? The type is rare, but it's not unknown. In this country, you find a similar combination in Hector de Saint-Denys-Garneau and Robert Bringhurst, to name just two. Casting a wider net, I think of Snyder, Merton, Hopkins, John of the Cross as examples of the type.

But Lilburn is his own man, and there's no need to strain for comparisons. Where he will go next is anybody's guess. Meanwhile, we have *Living In The World As If It Were Home* to be grateful for.

Dennis Lee

PREFACE

Moosewood Sandhills, the Quill Lakes, the South
Saskatchewan River from Pike Lake to Fish Creek,
bush land north of Sault Ste. Marie: these places have
spoken this book. They are all useless land, too sandy,
too salty, too full of deadfall to hold the
entrepreneurial look, the remodelling gaze. They make
breathing easier. Human thinking hardly comes here;
the land is turned away, forgotten, blurred, curled in.
Origen speaks of apokatastasis, the restoration of all
things; I want to go back to the old world of the first
place. The project to convert what is into product
heaves forward almost everywhere; almost everything
seems caught in the beam of this attention. While this
goes on, I'll go down to the river; I'll look. These
essays consider what work might have to be done in
order to live in the world as if it were home. My hunch
is that the way to this is by the lunge of eros and by
looking.

*

The essays that follow were written over nine years.
They lean on one another; they repeat themselves;
they worry a small collection of knots.

A person needs companions for the journey. Mine have come mostly from the western monastic tradition and from the school of negative theology stretching from Gregory of Nyssa and Gregory of Nazianzen through pseudo-Dionysius the Areopagite to the author of *The Cloud of Unknowing*.

I wanted to return from the exile of all my previous looking and wondered how this could be done.

*

I use an unusual language in places, a language coming from this old tradition. I do this not to be hidden but to touch what now appears to be out of range. Contemporary terms, had I been able to find anything remotely suitable, would have been inevitably reductive. They would have been unmusical, no ear in them for what the old words gesture toward.

*

This book is part of conversations I have been having over several years with friends: Jan Zwicky, Don McKay, Dennis Lee, Susan Shantz. Had I no one to talk to, I likely would have had nothing to say.

Jan Zwicky's *Lyric Philosophy* has been an orienting book; it led me to be bold. Zdravko Planinc and his book *Plato's Political Philosophy* taught me how to read Plato.

I thank the Saskatchewan Arts Board, the Canada Council and the Ontario Arts Council for their assistance during the time in which these essays were written.

I am not interested in theology but in desire. Traditionally, however, the sort of erotic experience that draws me has been cast either in Christian theological language or in the dialectical language of Plato. The eros for the world, I believe, unfolds in the same way as dialectic and the eros for God have been understood to unfold.

How
To Be
Here?

— Moosewood Sandhills —

Deer come out of the poplars just as day becomes
night; they move in the blue air. Dropped grain near
the house glistens in the hollow they've licked and
stamped over the weeks into snow. Their bodies are
dense with strangeness and are weightless, brief
electric arcs on the eye, eloquent, two does faring well
this winter, bow-sided, v-faced, coming down the
slope through low willow and wild rose that holds the
last of light. They stop repeatedly, their coloratura
caution; their bodies seem the constant, quavering
afterglow of this strained attention. Yet the gold of the
grain pulls the goldenness of them. They come the last
steps quickly along a path notched with their prints
from nights before and bend to eat. Shadow soaks into
them. One of them jerks up a look, then the other.
They see me standing by the woodpile. They stare. I
stare.

Consciousness walks across the land bridge of the
deer's stare into the world of things. This is knowing.
It tastes of sorrow and towering appetite. Their look
seems a bestowal; I feel more substantial, less
apologetic as a physical thing from having been seen.
The traded look goes on in the building dark. There is
no intention here, nothing of fairy tale or hagiography,

animals lying down with the solitary, animals bearing
messages, scrolls caught in the clefts of their hoofs.
There is only wild seeing, the feel of it unimaginable:
I am seen straight through (of that, no doubt) but
cannot say how I am seen. Travelling back through the
conductor of this gaze, something of me, a slant I'd
never guess, enters them. Their look has a
particularity, an inexpressibility, so highpitched it
attracts myths. No wonder some say the darkness of
the forest is a god.

When consciousness crosses the divide into the
wilderness of what is there, it expects to find a point
of noetic privilege: at last a clear view into the heart of
things. But what it does find on the other side is
further peculiarity, a new version of distance. The deer
bend again to eat, then again nod up a stare. The world
is a collection of oddnesses, things so gathered into
themselves, so ruthlessly at home and separate, they
seem to shine with difference — poplar, these does,
wild roses. The weirdness, unreachability of things, is
not abolished by any sudden aberration of intimacy,
fluked into being by a deer's look, but is intensified by
it. The desire to feel otherness as selfhood, to be the
deer seeing yourself, remains; for me it never leaves,
the old residue of Paradise, that amicable common life
desire seems to remember, the old bone it never quits
gnawing. Nor does language's impulse to shrug off
this distance vanish. Yet both are qualified by the
unyielding unlikeness of specific things.

Looked at by the does in the falling light, I am
"seen home", attended closer to the centre of what is,
deked from a stance of noetic propriety, an heirloom
of spirit soberly passed on to me, the mind's fine
aloofness from bodies. The long stare is the occasion
of a loss of cognitive rectitude, a debauch in the low

life of objects. But at home through the other's look, the things of home seem even more deeply themselves, "known" are further enclaustered in idiosyncrasy. The opposite of objective removal from the world is not subjective union but an intensely felt differentiation. The deer show out from around the word "deer" and they have no name.

The world is its names plus their cancellations, what we call it and the undermining of our identifications by an ungraspable residue in objects. To see it otherwise, to imagine it caught in our phrases, is to know it without courtesy, and this perhaps is not to know it at all. To see with presumption is only to note the effects of one's bright looks, the glimmering classifications, the metaphors, is merely to watch oneself confidently gazing. The Franciscan John Duns Scotus said individuality was intrinsically intelligible, though perhaps not to us in our present state — in the body, after the Fall. Perhaps never, perhaps to no one. Perhaps individuality is not to be known, only lived with, each haecceitas helping to shape the other by its proximity. The desire to belong to what the deer belongs to, the wildness, the thereness, is mortified but remains true. You crane forward into the world in appetite and enter it in sorrow knowing that this good desire that casts you out of yourself is right and must not be lost but is necessarily and sharply frustrated.

*

All poets are liars, say people in West Africa; the praise-singers inflate your life without shame as they greet you at your door and chant you into your day. But poetry's audacity, its appetite for embellishment, makes it elastic in its accommodations of awe, makes it home to a sweep of the most extravagant human desires. More than any other speech, poetry is tolerant of a nostalgia for Paradise. Indeed, it may help to create as well as abet this eros, launching a series of fabulous plots for returning consciousness to the world. Its vector and velocity is desire leaning into the unknowable individuality of things; poetry is the artifact of this desire. Around everything is an epidermis of narrative, a layer of hypotheses, orders, causal grids by which the world is rendered intelligible. Poetry's fundamental appetite is ecstatic; its curiosity yearns beyond this barrier of intelligibility to know the withinness of things.

The knowledge poetry seeks is the most intimate, the names it aspires to utter those which its subjects, the deer, dogwood, new moon, would intone if they stood to sing. Poetry is consciousness dreaming of domicile at the core of the foreign world, the mind deeply homesick and scheming return, the tongue contorting itself toward uttering what such a return might be like. It is mind remembering the old world of the Garden, what it was there to be rarefied, translucent flesh, flesh so fine it was intelligence; being as self-consciousness; an emanation of reaching eros like stones, petals, fronds, but *thinking,* thought like a plume or rack of light. The lit tip of what is, life adorned with the plumage of awareness, mind as display, flesh spreading an invisible tail and strutting in the soft humid place of beginning: poetry remembers. Poetry leans into the world and back to this state when the mind bespoke the souls of things, gave them back as reflections in a peculiar pool. In poetry, the mind remembers itself as a prelapsarian thing that thought as others gave scent.

But poetry contorts the world it utters with good desire. It is prone to be "beautiful and yet very untrue". It can foster "falseness in all our impressions of external things". So Ruskin assails the "pathetic fallacy" in Volume III of *Modern Painters*. Poets, he complains, frequently imagine what is not there, supposing actual qualities "entirely unconnected with any real power or character of the object, and only imputed to it by us." Poetry is liable to visit sense on the world, to recast nature in pre-determined modes: poetry's version of knowing is a style of expectation. This involves, in Ruskin's view, making the external world more like us, flower, rock outcrops invested with emotional lives in consonance with the poet's own.

What is the source of this impulse to colonize the world psychically, bending otherness into human forms? Violent feelings, says Ruskin, poets "over-clouded with emotion". Such feelings — one of them, he implies, is an intense love for the world — are, however, laudable, even though they lead to falsity, a shrinking of the object to invention. Even the poet of "the first order", Ruskin's idealized creature, his heroic truth-seeker, *must* succumb to this fallacy on occasion or be "inhuman and monstrous". A capacity for Ruskin's fallacy, then, is a mark of virtue in this exemplar: "there are always some subjects which ought to throw him off his balance; some by which his poor human capacity for thought should be conquered and brought into the inaccurate and vague state of perception, so that the language of inspiration becomes broken, obscure and wild in metaphor." What leads poetry to misrepresent the world is poetry's capacity to be ravished by the world. The erroneous way poetry is wont to behold nature is morally necessary, therefore — "monstrosity" is the alternative to falling into "the inaccurate and vague state of perception" on certain subjects — and somehow true. To not be lifted out of oneself by certain things is to not be human.

One of these things, says Ruskin, is the presence of what seems to be a numinous élan in the world, what fires astonishment, shards of a cosmic grace stressed into singular things. Hopkins calls this "inscape", his word for describing what intimations of Scotus' haecceitas felt like on the palate of the keen eye, the elegance, for him, of the universal eased incredibly into this and that as idiosyncratic individuality. Before this, language ceases to name, breaks up, becomes, as a last resort, solipsistic. The world awakens awe, poplar, blond grass over snow, but when we come to characterize what it is in things that does this we stumble and fabricate. Poetry seems to be the speech of a desire, a love, an eros for union with the world building from awe, whose satisfaction poetry can achieve only by misrepresenting the world.

Poetry misconstrues what it loves, then, because it loves it. Sometimes poetry is electric with caritas and invests things liberally with an equality to consciousness because the world seems so delicate before the monomania of technology: you offer it the subsidy of human lifeblood; you enfranchise it with human quirks (think of Galway Kinnell or Don McKay). Or the woodlot and false solomon seal are seeded with emotion the better to reap the comfort from them that consciousness, in its loneliness for things, seeks. Then there's self-revulsion; anything is better than us; things alone are estimable (you see this in Lawrence's "Snake"). Or there's an anticipatory apokatastatic joy that occasionally quivers up in lyric, a celebration of the restoration of the union of all things, existing, in crude caricature, in imagination, present in desire, but yet-to-come in fact, that skews the recalcitrant difference of things. Or in some poetry there are traces of an incompletely formed contrition, an obeisance performed before objects, an offering to them of human traits in reparation for wounds consciousness' separation has inflicted on them, a compunctious refusal to insist upon any supremacy of the human, a truce imposed by the generosity of words. Language's quickness to overcome the conflict between person and world, its inadvertence to the extreme difficulty of this, its solicitude for the homeless mind, causes it to reduce being utterly to its names.

These yearnings at home in poetry — to courtesy to the world, to apokatastasis, to contrition — are right, attractive like Ruskin's "violent feelings", but cannot be met in poetry. They must be schooled in order to find their proper satisfaction, and this schooling must take place mostly outside of language. If poetry is the artifact of such desires, it gestures toward an enterprise beyond poetry. Language as well must be schooled if the desires poetry sequesters are to be fulfilled. For language, unqualified by awe before the unspeakable otherness of deer and poplar, language unhurt by wonder, confects a union between self and world that seems right, the summation of yearning, but that in fact asserts this separation with fresh force by making what is vanish in caricature. Poetry is the rearing in language of a desire whose end lies beyond language.

*

How to be here? The land is thin, coyote-bony,
sandhills with low juniper cover, chokecherry scrub
with oatgrass, crested wheat, a little brome, thickets
dark in snow, a flickering place. Bones of old herds
are sways of shadowy light under the blond earth; the
Milky Way smokes over dead, glimmering winter
grass. The land looks like scraped hide, bits of hair
still tufted to it. Diamond willow, dogwood — there
are deer tracks everywhere in the groves, in this white,
blank place, the dry land, pale place to which the dead
were once believed to meander, the faint, slow hills.
Its scrawniness, lostness, shrugs off the casual look,
anything light, any look with its gravity elsewhere, a
shy land, yet strict, alkaline. How to be here in the last
years of a hard century?

One is lofted by desire into the world. How to be
here? When monks first left the rich abbey at
Molesmes in 1098 and came to Cîteaux intending "to
pursue heavenly studies" and seek, in that extreme
time, a stricter application of Benedict's rule, they
noted with delight that the country they entered was "a
place of horror, a vast wilderness" that seemed to
"hear" their religious hunger. Where else to be now
but in these deer-coloured, long grass hills, cactus
lands, in the margins of the age? This is a good place
to take one's time in, watch, crane into the distance of
things. There are pools of iron water sunk below the
base of the hills. This is a good place to learn sorrow,
luctus, what the old monks called penthos, a bleak
place to enact a politics of silence and solitude, the
grouse-taupe, knobby land.

How to be with the deer that see you at evening
and do not stir, the poplar, wolf willow clumps, the
ghosts of this place? How to enter the wilderness of
discrete things? I could write about it, have written

poems about it, but this has set me beyond writing. The place seems frail; the merest invention could make it disappear. How to know this land without vanquishing it? Poetry gestures to contemplation and contemplation feeds the poetry, modifying language by letting awe undermine it, pare it back, lending the poems a thinness, compunction. This is a land to wait in, watching. Bring anonymity; namelessness has a place here; the land worn to the bone hints into you an interior mimesis of namelessness. Bring sorrow. Watch.

Last summer I slept on the bare land in a saucer the wind had worried into the sand of a glacial spillway; it is filled now with snowberries and fescue. Below me needle grass roots drifted fifteen feet into soil, nuzzling for small water. Below them, broadcasts of bones curved through the earth. Above the quill-coloured hollow, and a nearby alfalfa field grown in tight with crested wheat, were the salt flats of the moon. Saskatoons were a week away from picking; their watery smell smudged the air. I wanted to know what the wildness would put in my dreams, what the grass roots, working water from below, would lift into my sleep. I dreamt a woman of wonderful weight, like an African market mama, a quarter the size of night; she drew vast breasts from her darkness, one then the other and rested them on a table before her; each was heavy as dogma. This is what's at stake, I dream-thought, the issue. Later, waking, I realized the dream could mean anything or nothing. The issue of what?

Toward fall, the stars were brighter. I went to a gathering of poplars on a hill tip deeper in the long grass, bleached place, where the juniper was thick, a hidden-away, curled-in spot no one visits, where the deer go when the hunters start moving up and down the roads. I wanted to watch. The hills were burly with old heat, the grass was uncountable, muscular, a tabulation of some variety beyond me. I lay down in the night dampness below the bone-glare of starlight. Be awake, listen, forget yourself. The mosquitoes were bad and I came home. There is something out there, other, its strangeness beautiful, wooing, unnameable, delectable.

There is the contemplation of the physical world, said the monks of the Egyptian desert, and the contemplation of God; each is part of a single eros. The contemplation of God, they said, was a helpless, desire-filled gaze into what could not be known, a concentration of desire craning toward the unreachable source of being. Contemplation of the physical world, theoria physike, yields "true knowledge of existing things", said Evagrius Ponticus, monk, Platonist, in his *Praktikos*, yields the true gnosis of created beings, their essence, logoi (*Praktikos*, 2). The labour that precedes this seeing, that is, in fact, this knowing, is the same, I think, as the preparation peculiar to the contemplation of supramundane things, involves the same subversions of ideas and language. "What is a monk?" someone asked the old man John the Dwarf in the wastes of Scetis. "He is toil," the abba replied. The monk is poured into waiting, watching and tears, the ascesis contemplative knowing calls forth, the thinning of self, the building and focusing of desire.

Contemplation grows out of the wreckage of other forms of knowing, other forms of being, is, in part, their wreckage. Language breaks up in it, identity breaks up, consolation is disassembled. The contemplative pulls away from what is untoward, what is implausibly certain in his knowing to bring it to light. All early authorities on monastic gnosis insist a period of ascetical denial precedes the toil of contemplation but it is true, as well, that the impulse to know the world contemplatively ends in asceticism, that knowing can be this dampening of self, that the pursuit of ascetical virtue and knowledge are co-terminous. The desire to know the world behind its names is the death of knowing which is objective, ordering, communicable and of the apparently secure life that rests on such knowing.

13

The physical world cannot be known in the way poetry aspires to know it, intimately, ecstatically, in a way that heals the ache of one's separation from the world, it seems to me, outside of the sundering of knowledge which contemplation is. And contemplation's knowing is not a knowing at all, offers nothing clear and distinct, nothing sure, universal. The contemplative does not retreat from the world with a knowledge enriched with names for things, a mental map of efficient causalities. Yet in contemplation one loves the world and wants to be in the world in love without skewing it.

Contemplation of nature, like contemplation of God in negative theology, is a knowing which is an unknowing, a frustration of the desire to know in which, nevertheless, this desire persists, heightened, hurtling one forward into the unknowability of unique things. The knowing of discrete things, these sandhills, the rose hollows, chokecherry tufts dark in snow, the deer, is a not-knowing of them, a humbling of the mind's workaday cravings for fixity, certitude, while one persists in desiring to know them.

You are impoverished by contemplation. Whatever self-sufficiency you can claim, your flattering distance from things, the consolation of being in control, are all shaken. This impoverishment is, in part, the knowing contemplation achieves — the human self quelled, domesticated to dwell in the world. As the mind leans into the darkness of God, the old writers said, it is slendered by awe, reduced to a good confusion: this is knowing. Language, as well, is chastened in contemplation and by being broken it provides a way by which the unspeakable may be approached. There are two paths, said early mystical writers, the via positiva and the via negativa, the way of light and the way of darkness. Affirmative theology, the way of light, is an understanding of the divine nature as it is exposed in the intelligible orders of being; one declares, tracking the divinity in ekstasis, that the source of being is good, intelligent, beautiful and so on. In negative theology, however, they said, a richer knowledge of the divine nature comes, the intimate knowledge of human ecstasy, a no-knowledge. You are drawn "with your understanding laid aside, to strive upward . . . to the ray of the divine shadow which is above" all affirmations and denials to a knowing superior to all "rational and intellectual activities" says the pseudo-Dionysius in his *The Mystical Theology* (1000A). This theology is a path of disorientation, muting and appetite ending in conjunction with being's apex. On it, all names for the divinity are rejected as inadequate: God is not good if by this one would constrain the divine in images of human beneficence, nor just if one has in mind mere human justice. God is supra-goodness, beauty beyond beauty, No-thing. Some of the same cancellations occur as one edges toward the brome grass head, the porcupine faced at the foot of the drive in grey false dawn, in their unknowable otherness. Language is sundered as one courts ecstasy into the gazing deer who, at the same time, in some unguessable way, are perhaps being ecstasied into oneself.

I walk in the hills in winter. A sharptail grouse explodes from drift-fold where she's hidden from the cold, her feces bunched around her. I am going into the hills where the deer in February browse juniper. Lost place, the original grass cover has never been broken. The snow would come to mid-thigh if I stepped from my snowshoes. The ground is blank except for some fox or coyote tracks; once, last winter, I saw an ermine out this way. I walk through heavy poplar, each grove rhizoming from the first tree of the bush, ghost wood, smelling like stale bread when you cut through it. I come over the rise and there are the deer, standing in the pits they've hoofed into the snow to get at juniper tips. They do not see me. I look beyond them, further south, more poplar bush, hills, an old fence line, willow in the hollows, still: nothing. How to name this land? It's a skellig, black rock in the Atlantic. It's a half-scraped hide. What does it speak in memory? What titles to give it in a praise-singing? Language again and again springs at the essence, reaching for clarity, the exact fit between the look of the slow hills, occultly breathing and their feel, then denies each time what it comes up with. The land is the gold-tipped pelt of deer. It is the topography of Tibetan chant. It is a bone-land; it is the glittering place beloved by the nomadic dead. Language asserts and cancels itself, names the world then erases the name, and in this restlessness one glimpses the aptness of confusion before the ungraspable diversity of here. Silence. The look goes on. The breaking up of language, language drawn into the reversal of language, is the speech of desire beating against the silence of the confusing land.

Individuality, specificity, haecceity — the thisness of a thing that makes it unlike all others, its final perfection, its beauty, godlikeness — lies beneath order, law, name. The deer, the one nearest me, has no name; she is perfect unlikeness and is known best when desire leans into the cloud of her, as names assemble and withdraw around her. She merits all these — body of lightning, gold-tipped, decorous — but is known best beyond them, known in a silence momentumed with the intention and velocity of desire. Beat with a naked intent upon the cloud of your unknowing, advises an anonymous fourteenth-century author. Lean into the world with appetite to know it, batten yourself to it, desire passing through the brokeness of language, language bespeaking this desire by dismantling itself.

Contemplation's impulse is to understand the world. It is not a romantic confection, not a self-consoling gape at chimerae, but inquiry into being where the truth of being, being as unutterably particular or unutterably universal, lies past the certainty language assembles. It is a form of knowing that strains across the distance between mind and world and aims to end in union with what it seeks. But what is union with something that can't be known, the deer, ideas in the mind of the divine? It is a standing alongside, an affective nudging against, a dwelling-at-a-distance-with, a beating with a naked intent. The thisness of the nearest doe bent over the juniper, her transfixing oddness, is the littling of language, mortification of the desire for clarity, yet an occasion of the love which is one shape of contemplative attention. The eros to know the deer, as you encounter her unknowable particularity, resolves itself into — fails into — a pressing, unrequited fondness that waits before her; this knowledge is the beginning of fidelity, a bedding down with things. It is mind finding a frail home in the garden of otherness. *figurative*

*

We are lonely for where we are. Poetry helps us cope. Poetry is where we go when we want to know the world as lover. You read a poem or write one, guessing at the difficult, oblique interiority of something, but the undertaking ultimately seems incomplete, ersatz. The inevitable disappointment all poems bring motions toward the hard work of standing in helpless awe before things. "The praise of the psalms is a lament" the old men and women of the desert used to say. Poetry in its incompleteness awakens a mourning over the easy union with the world that seems lost. Poetry is a knowing to this extent: it brings us to this apposite discomfiting.

The earliest Western monks, Evagrius, John the Dwarf, Anthony — there was unanimity in the cells on this — said that ascesis, the self-abnegation of fasting, vigils, chastity, preceded contemplative deepening. You wept your way into the presence of the numinous. You took up combat with your "passions" to achieve a degree of the quiet which ascetical virtue could bring, and then you were capable of contemplation. The attitude of mourning ascesis fostered was what the knowing of that which lay beyond reason and language felt like, they said. Without disagreeing with this, I believe as well that contemplation creates its own ascetical experience: contemplative looking involves a slendering of self.

Language, yes, is bent back on itself in contemplation: you sense that the sort of noetic intimacy you reach for — grasping *this* tree as this tree in its complex eccentricity — lies beyond speech, even with language's impressive energy for praise, praise that the beauty of what is detonates out of it. Beyond praise is lament; the fact of the thing is still far away. Desire, as well, is brought up short in contemplation. The eros that makes poems and is nursed in poems is for the union of consciousness with the world, the abrogation of humanity's expulsion from the Garden. But how does the mind imagine this union? What does it suppose this dwelling in the other, this ecstasy, feels like? Typically it casts the satisfaction of this desire as a possession of a thing by absorption in it; I become the deer and they are turned into mine. Or perhaps union is conceived as a galvanizing penetration of a thing, an entry into otherness won by the projectile force of my curious gaze, and the acquisition of its secrets, trophies which bring me peace, the end of noetic-affective striving. Desire for the other, return to the world, imagined in either of these ways, is chastened in contemplation. Contemplated, the deer never loses her distance, unlikeness; if anything she becomes arrestingly darker. But the observer, led by his desire, is altered, changed into a figure of hunger, leaning without break into the wonderful peculiarity of the specific thing. Desire for the world, mortified by contemplation, is desire whose satisfaction is its frustration and continuance. Contemplative knowing is not a feeling, a rest, a peace that sweeps over one, reward for the ferocity of one's romantic yearnings, one's energetic Wordsworthian peerings. Contemplative knowing of the deer and the hill must gather about the conviction that neither can be known. It is the resolute taking of a stance before the world, a positioning of oneself in desire-filled unknowing before the hill and deer, that refuses all hope of consolation.

But the ascesis contemplation urges on us goes deeper than even negations of speech and desire. The monks of the desert believed that the contemplative grasp of what is hidden required the assistance of the body, was impossible if the body was not in consonance with the mind's aspirations. "Howl, weep, moan and bring the soul back to God," exhorts Ephrem the singer, Syrian, fourth century. Since coming to these hills, the dark hollows of grass, I have felt a need to let the reversals contemplation triggers in thought and language find expression in my skin. I have wanted to mime unknowing. So I slept in the hills under summer stars, wanting little to protect me from the night and blue-green ground. Deny whatever affirms your elevation from the world of things, I urged myself, with no clear notion of what I was after. Last winter, I sat near deer beds for hours, watching, not for deer especially, intent, posted, yet unfocused. Late last August, I dug a hole in the south face of a hill, a place to be intruded on by dreams, a place in which to wait. I dug seven feet down into the slope; it took me three weeks. I found curiously rounded stones and an arc of old bones a little lower. I poured footings, set in place thick insulated walls, added a roof of straw bales and buried the structure. A four inch black plastic air pipe now protrudes from the resodded earth. The room smells mealy, of damp, of shavings. The sand floor is a pool of silence; it seems permeable; it invites a further digging. I tell people the place is a root cellar, and I do have some potatoes in it, but it feels also like a listening station, a place where, sitting and attending, I can inquire into the darkness of what I miss. I'll wait here; I could be living on a pillar.

Ascesis is a gathering and narrowing of self. It springs
from an appetite for delight; it angles toward virtue.
Procrustean versions of this, physical and emotional
self-mutilations, asceticism as it's popularly imagined
and has often been practised, are corrupt forms
coming from coarse readings of Plato, wacky zeal, or
grumpiness around the ignoble limitations of daily
life, a self-grandeur, a literal love for the impossibly
heroic. This sort of angelistic contempt for human
things has more to do with a rich, triumphalistic
narcissism than with obeying the impulses
contemplation provokes in you. It lacks, as the old
ones would say, discernment. Asceticism, in truth, is
being sped by the wish to be singlehearted. You draw
yourself into the channel of one eros. Other
enticements are allowed to atrophy, especially ones
that are ultimately enervating, vainglory, anger, a taste
for lassitude, power. One assembles focus, weight,
momentum, is hurtled toward delight. It is a
homecoming, a return to one's most rudimentary
desire. I felt this drift working dimly in me as I dug
the hole, a sweet motion, a ghostly rocking.

You find yourself emptying by increments to
receive the impress of things. The root of asceticism
thus conceived is ravishment by objects; you are
silenced by the gleam of their oddness, turned-away-
ness. What does it mean to become nothing? someone
once asked a good man in the desert. "It means to
place oneself beneath irrational things and to know
that they are without blame." Let the importance of
the world totter pomp. Retrieve all names, assertions
of similarity, the world of the slight glance, of course
— this happens when you look hard — but refuse,

further, the allure of posturings justified by the old hierarchies. Wait in the hole; wait along deer paths; keep your eyes open. What do you amount to, after all? You want just one thing: to know the world so you can go back to it. Let the way the golden bean, wolf willow, snowberry, the deer present themselves to you be seeing them. Let the deer look at you and let this be seeing. I say all this to myself. The mutedness, foldedinness, of this position is a precursor of a deferent courtesy to being, and this courtesy, growing from an experience of ravishment, is a knowing of things, in which one leans in aroused attention into them, a dwelling with, a pressing alongsideness, a vivifying beguilement.

This sort of seeing, a seeing poetry gestures toward, a seeing which is a being touched by the world, musters in you a particular stance. This stance becomes the buttressing context for contemplation, becomes the contemplation itself. It is a stance of quiet before things in which your various acquisitivenesses — for knowledge, supremacy, consolation — are stilled, exhausted before the remoteness, the militant individuality of what is there. It is a stance of being alert without anticipating anything, a slackening of self which is a higher form of intensity. Dig a hole in the earth, lie in it, wait. It is a giving up which is an expression of a desire for everything. It may involve vigils, fasts, the undertaking of a long looking without expectations that feels like a vow fulfilment, divinatory sleeps. It requires the renunciation of all secret pleasures that cosset consciousness in its estrangement from the physical world, like the delectable satisfaction of having something to look down on, the attractiveness of which to us is our estrangement. How to know the thisness of things, their hectic complexity, their strangeness, cool otherness? These things can be praised or they can be viewed with longing. But the gaze is best, most authentic, when rooted in a posture of deference and attention. This stance must be cultivated. Such cultivation is asceticism and it is one with knowing. It involves submitting to be disarmed and taking on the silence of things, the marginality and anonymity of grass, sage, lichen, things never properly seen.

22

The world ignites awe. Language heats, grows ejaculatory, protean, physical as it takes on the energies of song; it denies what it asserts because it is in love with what it names. An exhaustion sets in; awe persists; a desire to simply look springs up around the lunges of language. One gazes at the world with alacrity and courtesy and becomes less. Look long enough, faithfully enough at the tree, your seeing a bowing before it, let the deer's stare seep deeply into you, and you lose your name. Eventually a contemplative stance toward the world comes to mourning. Weep at your separation from what is; the mind as prodigal touches bottom and in its recognition of its poverty recovers itself. One does miss the homeland of being where one is. Such mourning, however, is perhaps what knowing the world and being in it, with awareness, is. It asserts the enormity of being and the vast intricacy of individual things, their beauty, their difference from us. It demonstrates an awareness of consciousness' removal from wild things and its consequent ransacking of them. It is a form of reparation. You grieve and this is a way into things and home. In this awareness of things' oddness and in your compunction over your separation from this is a letting-be-of-the-world while you are turned fully toward it. This is a return, fretful, likely to be checked, mind finding its place among scents, grass tips, bloom colours, a tremor of an act building from a quick desire that mysteriously never fully abandons you.

Contemplation

And

Cosmology

— Batchawana Bay —

A mile out in the gigantic lake, far past bay mouth, ice ends in tall turquoise dunes against which the surf piles and builds, piles and builds. Fox move on the white river at night. Twelve feet of snow have fallen in the dark and pale trees this winter; you go nowhere without snowshoes once off the ploughed road. Look, look well — the astounding particularity of things entices the careful love-attention of contemplation. This is the theoria physike of the early desert monks, Anthony, Evagrius, others. Contemplation is inquiry into the nature of being; it is not amelioration practised by the credulous, not a shirking of the adult task of intentional activity. It is silence in response to the utterly human exigent vocation: understand the world.

But how understand? Contemplation's attention-in-silence knows by standing alongside, craning toward, dwelling with. Its knowing is poor: it doesn't draw back from its subject bearing the extracted wealth of an essence, a meaning, a moral. Contemplation is the moment when human knowing, lured by the possibility of perfect understanding, is thwarted, shamed, bent back on itself, but continues to know through this shame. Contemplation is knowledge impoverished and embarrassed but that keeps going. This knowing in the midst of the embarrassment of knowledge topples into adoration. Adoration has the completeness for contemplation that judgment has for rational inquiry. Contemplation, unlike the more entrepreneurial noesis of analytic reason, is not interested in the power of knowledge over the thing known, not interested in converting it to utility: marvelling is exactly enough.

Contemplation is a stance, a holding oneself in visual and mental readiness before the world which is not a mirror, not a problem, an adversary, friend, playground, not "raw stuff", not symbol, not a balm, not a terror. The contemplative must be disciplinedly poor: you must stand before your subject, attention straining, convinced you know nothing. You do not presume to name, define; the task is simply to look in "perfect" puzzlement at the birch branch, the river, the stone, the lake, to dwell in each with alert unknowing. Contemplation is the desire for something finer than the pleasure of regarding one's imagination caught in the act of naming. It is the taste for ecstasy of reverence, the mind feeling all names fumble from it, the feel of the truth of that.

Contemplation's vector is transcendental yet it bends as well into the world. There its subject is individualities, thisnesses. Contemplation knows the world as a spectacle of difference in which each thing is nothing other than its inscrutable self. It attends to things so finely themselves they fall beneath order, law. Look out the window: a birch tree, a frozen river mouth behind, the slowly rotting ice pack of the bay, green-brown cliffs of an old mountain range. Look closely at the birch, a branch halfway up it. The branch gropes toward you like an intuition reaching impossibly toward clarity. What is the music-like chaos in the twigs of this birch branch in winter? Here is a stupendous manyness of shape, angle, colour — grey, black, plum, brown, ivory. You can stumble and stare all morning at this branch. What is the order here, the sense, intelligibility: how to think about this branch? What is it like? How come to rest with this branch, its antlering muchness? The questions gradually become less insistent, less outraged. Knowing is still thwarted, still stumbling and staring, but now you have an inkling of the shapeliness of your incomprehension. Stay with it and the carefully attentive befuddlement unravels into a fidelity to the branch, a setting down of stakes, an alongside-ness, a fretful proximity to the branch that is as far as it can be known. The frustration of knowing the whatness of the branch while you persist in singleminded, full-bodied attention to it is the contemplative knowing of this particular branch.

Contemplation is gazing at the birch tree, or the river, or the lake with a muddled heart and an insistent noetic desire: understand the world. The further you press this desire in silence, the darker your intellect becomes. Contemplation's knowing is unknowing. Its understanding is apophatic. Apophasis for the early monk-theologians of the Christian West was the highest understanding, the only true way to comprehend what in the world awoke human awe. The word "apophasis" suggests denial, a noughting of self, intellect and language that occurs when these, impelled by yearning, press to achieve their fullest expression, the darkness into which they ultimately flower. Such desire-filled unknowing, for the earliest Western contemplatives, was the route to the most intimate cosmology. The apophatic knowledge of the contemplative is the essence of the via negativa; for later writers like Gregory of Nyssa, pseudo-Dionysius the Areopagite and Maximus the Confessor, it was the core of the "dark" mystical path to a relationship with the heart of the universe. The deepest truth in all things is numinous, the apophatic writers said, beyond reason, beyond language. It is not exactly true to say that the source of life is good, for that power that vitalizes and informs all things is goodness beyond goodness, supra-goodness, they said. And even if the mind could grasp what this superlative quality seemingly was, they believed, it would be lured eventually to cancel this notion as caricature. Knowing in the apophatic tradition is an attentive, name-cancelling darkness of mind, a darkness dazzling with noetic passion. The language of this tradition typically describes the soul's approach to God; it can be used, I believe, too, to plot the return of consciousness to the world, unnameable in its athletic variety.

Apophatic knowledge is not quietism, an emptying of mind. It is a naming of things beyond names, a naming which continuously overwhelms itself in a headlong appetite for the object, a desire-filled inquiry rushing past its momentary certainties into wonder. The birch branch is an intuition meandering endlessly toward a clear idea. No, it is music: fifty violin concerti locked in gangling wood a chasm-like spark-gap from the ear. It echoes the profusion of stars. No, it is like the complication, the odd-angledness of bird song. Silence — the gaze going on, a probing. Apophasis is a naming which unnames itself: approximates then overcomes the guess while still retaining it because the truth lies through language in language's brokenness. None of the names is as true as the rhythm of naming then cancelling the name in quest of a further aptness that woos the mind with even more insistence.

All this leads to wonder, but a wonder that is plucked, worried by distraction. This is a maintaining of the contemplative look, its self-effacement, leaping energy, no matter the temptation to desert it, including the temptation to abandon the whole task because it seems so un-wonder-like. Wonder is an ascesis, a discipline chosen, an election not a grace: I stand this way before the world naming, name denying, attending, intending in love — a noesis that senses in its imperfection the possibility of perfection. Wonder is not thrilling, not enlightenment, not a flash, not a marvellous evacuation of images from the mind, not a confident feeling of oneness with the branch, the river, the green mountains. It is more homely, ragged, less ravished, exigent, capable of devotion. It is a style of holding oneself before the world resulting from an apprehension that the world cannot be known otherwise, cannot be known unless one lays down the task of knowing it while retaining the desire to know it.

All contemplation becomes apophatic as it deepens. All of it names then sublates the name, glimpsing dimly that the truest knowing of the subject — God or this particular birch branch — lies in the desire to be in constant and unfailingly imperfect quest of it. All contemplation is a knowing which is an unknowing, a darkness in mind caused by an excess of light in the object, a superlative attractiveness, a beckoning energy, complex individuality. Contemplative knowing does not seek the same epistemological mastery as reason, does not imagine that a thing known is one that rests easily in the palm of the mind, caught in description, known in its rough similarity to other things. Contemplation lets fall names, eschews power, to clear the ground for astonishment; it revels in eccentricity. It does not wish to subdue the world but to dwell in it. Apophatic knowledge thus chastens itself in order to complete itself, stilling the impulse for noetic facility to achieve the far more attractive quality of an interior courtesy toward being. Contemplative courtesy is not mere respect for the natural world. Strength, ardour, gentleness, deference, magnanimity — the courteous silence of contemplation allows the mind to dwell with a graceful fretting in the world. The end of contemplation is not dominance or circumscription, but affective domesticity: the birch branch is not an item of knowledge but where I love, where my look rests in insistent and adoring incomprehension. I do not define the branch; it defines me by giving me a home. Knowledge is the generosity of being to the homeless mind.

Contemplation, apophasis, is a resting in the attractive idiosyncrasy of this river, this mountain, a homecoming to what is. But this rest is not static, stable or placid, is not a condition of epistemological privilege achieved by the earlier negations of language and elevated from contemplation's apophatic linguistic restlessness. Rather, it is a giving up before the variety of things, a thinning of self, a self-quelling that appears now and then in the midst of language's efforts to bespeak the unutterable singularity of things, an exhaustion in the company of this singularity. It is a desire-filled silence that is this speech continued. It resolves itself into an affection for the tree, the stone, a bedding down with them, a sense that their particularity is what gives one gravity and place in the world.

While contemplation involves the erasure of clear images and names and leans toward a thinking without images, a speech of silence, it nurses no cosy preference for obscurity. All knowing darkens as it builds. One presses against one's incomprehension with a seamless desire to know the subject in utter completeness. Beat constantly with a naked intent upon the cloud of your unknowing. Indeed, contemplation is a recovery of the full eros to know being clearly in all its specificity, to know the world as itself, unqualified by language, unedited by consciousness, to know it as it would be known by a perfect intellect. Such knowledge, at the moment, lies in silence, an attentive, name-asserting, name-cancelling silence. Here knowledge is love; knowledge is desire, the eros to know fully which is the eros for marriage to the world. You hold yourself mentally on the balls of your feet before the branch, the stone, caught by the beauty of the thing's difference, desiring its fullest comprehension, a union of self and branch, yet aware that your desire to know it in its full particularity will always be frustrated. Contemplation is the mind humbled and sharpened, made keen for love.

*

Apophatic teachers link the highest contemplative knowledge with virtue, the fruit of ascetical practice. Contemplation refuses any bifurcation of life and knowing. Approximation of virtue in one's approach to the world is a precondition of accurate knowledge; without it: fantasy, projection, the "cooking" of the subject to please preconception. A certain purity of heart grounds the noetic courtesy of contemplation.

This "abundance of virtue" is achieved by "laborious industry", said Maximus the Confessor. The ornate silence of contemplation rests in a disciplining of self, a channelling of eros. Let persons eager for contemplative knowledge "brighten by virtue of the ascetical force of the soul", let them put their affections in school, shape them toward the possibility of awe. "Finally through the altar of the mind" the contemplative "summons the silence abounding in song in the innermost recesses of the unseen and unknown utterance of the divinity by another silence rich in speech and tone" (*The Church's Mystagogy,* 4).

Maximus is speaking of a "way", a mode of holding oneself before what one would approach that precedes and accompanies a contemplative bedding down in the cosmos. Every mystical tradition advocates some program of self-discipline: only the pure see. This must not be confused with the self-mutilation of rectitude; it has nothing to do with a horror of flesh and feeling. Rather it is a schooling of eros leading to its unlimited enhancement. The "way" is hermeneutic: a means of comprehending what is incomprehensible, other — the chaos of colour and angle that is the winter branch, the perfect oddness of this particular stone half-covered in exactly this manner with fresh snow.

I saw an ikon once of a male figure in the Cathedral of St. John the Divine in New York City. The cheeks were ravined by tears; the whole face — even the skin and bones seemed absorbed in the look — took in some large sadness: the world? the loneliness of human life outside Paradise? The mourning of the face was exquisite, as graceful an epiphany of human nature as music. Here is the point of asceticism: you gather yourself in, amassing a density of attention, in order to bring your eros to what can evoke its length and breadth, depth and height: sorrow for the world, ravishment by the world, attention to splendour, attention to horror. The abnegation of the "way" is a stilling of other itches (for distraction, for approbation, for security) which deflect attention from the worthy enormities presented to mind, dwindle fundamental human eros to comfort.

The contemplation of birch branches and stones, the adoring look that freights the beholder to the world, the noetic stance of courtesy toward being, claims an ascetical practice. It requires a cognitive humility, a deference to the significance of being, a mortification of the intellect's will to power. You cannot truly see this stone if you believe the world is yours to do with as you will. Interiorly speaking, you must lay no violent hands upon it. Eros must be freed from the belittling impulse to convert the world into something useful or consoling and be brought to expend itself in its true delight: the contemplative look.

Cognitive humility entails a fasting of the intellect. You subdue the need for intellectual clarity and the security this brings, and take nourishment instead from the belief that the mere desire to know a thing in its vast thisness is to know it. "This truly is the vision of God: never to be satisfied in the desire to see him", observes Gregory of Nyssa. Contemplation of the branch means letting it be nothing other than what it really is, unqualified by intellect, almost eerie in its complete otherness. In contemplation, marvelling and questing to know is knowing.

Contemplation can require a disciplining of desires for closeness with the world. Mute the urge to achieve a bogus proximity to the world by remodelling it so it gains an easy welcome in the house of consciousness. The wilderness is not loved in the theme motel whose sign on the edge of the busy highway shows two smiling bears in neckties and fedoras. Leave the world solitary in its difference. Assume only a self-effacing intimacy with it, so that the closer you press toward the stone the more its unlikeness to you is underscored.

*

Contemplation rides an exigent wave of desire outward: understand the world. It is an exercise in ecstasy; it is an insistent gazing that bucks you from yourself into the world which then returns you to yourself, healed, restless, bereft. That's how contemplation understands, but what does it understand? What does attention-in-silence tell us about the real? How do its hints, glimmerings, contribute to cosmology?

Extreme variety is being's most alluring, wonder-wakening trait, an apparently limitless play of density, colour, grain, angle and thus it, more than anything, beckons the adoring look. Contemplation's subject, when it turns to the world, is the thisness, the uniqueness, the flamboyance of individual things. It tells us that the world in its immense specificity is unknowable but lovable: that it can be known only apophatically by the mind naming then reversing its names until it edges toward muted, protean regard. Contemplation further tells us that the cosmos can accommodate the most audacious human desire, the desire for the oneness of all things, that it is not hostile to a nostalgia for Paradise. It tells us that the splendour of being's difference quickens awe. It tells us that the world links itself to us through our awe, our awe the root system of being, sunk in the noosphere. It tells us that the truth of limitless particularity lies beneath language, but is accessible to language when language asserts then cancels itself, asserts, cancels. For in the restlessness of these reversals is the eros of the language-user to return home to his place among stones, river, maples. Contemplation tells us that the truth of the world is that it is a home for us, is the place-that-gives-a-home-to-the-eros-impelled-mind. It tells us that being, at least in part, is ecstatic: the contemplative is in the world by always travelling out of himself.

Contemplation's observations on cosmology are shy of clarity, of precise definition: they come with the loss of the desire to still the world in thought even as the mind continues to crane forward, toppling. Its knowledge of the world is like the slowly accreting "blood knowledge" by which the immigrant comes to feel at home in, be fed by, a new geography, a new culture. It is not quantifiable, teachable, marketable, cannot be commanded, but is indispensable: it is the learning of a relationship that nourishes, makes life possible. It is like the knowledge of acquiring a taste. The cosmology of contemplation is a gradually growing familiarity; its deepest truth is a feeling-at-homeness, a grateful silence. It is a loving, a dwelling in, a resting, a being defined by a place, a branch, a river, a stone, a mountain, a lake.

THE RETURN
TO THE
Garden

— Moosewood Sandhills —

What is the worth of the world? The world — owl
feathers scattered on the forest floor, seen at dusk —
has no worth. Or, worse, has a kind of anti-worth —
poplar cotton, the loft of the hills — coarsening the
soul with the weight of its consolations. The soul must
part with such things, the old, misguided
understanding goes; it must end its sad affair with the
body.

There has been a pattern of antipathy to physical
things in the Christian spiritual tradition: the soul is
the self and the soul's homeland is heaven. But this
renunciation has been equivocal. The world, after all,
is also the artifact of the Word, a second scripture:
something glitters in the muddle of what is there.

There also has been the conviction that there are
two sorts of things, one visible, the other unseen. The
unseen is by far the best of what is, uncompounded,
incorruptible, unchanging. It is what we know when
we truly understand: such knowledge is what
completes us as human beings. What is unseen is
enclosed in things, yet no hint of this presence reaches
the senses. These are arrested oddly by what falsifies
knowledge — transitory manifestations of this and
that in the flux of becoming and perishing. To follow

their lead is to become lost, "drunken" in soul — thus the importance of jettisoning them. The unseen informs owls, hills, sticks with whatever intelligibility they possess, holding them from chaos, and these occult essences disclose themselves to intelligence alone. Reason, the soul's noblest power, so this particular story goes, is uninterested in the beetle-like call of the clay-coloured sparrow, say, or the irregularities of wing-shadings among hawks, what the senses dote on; an impalpable fixity in objects attracts it, for the soul, it was said, is eternal and wants the company of what is invariant. The world has significance, then, only because of what it stolidly houses and obscures. You attend to it because it gives you inklings of a better place, your home, where your perfection awaits you. The Western religious regard for the world often seems to amount to an attention to the world that thrusts the world aside to grasp the presumed light within. It is a form of inadvertence; it is too composed; it is not quite credible; it looks wrong; it has no wildness in it.

*

Three summers ago, Maurice, a friend, took a plywood sheet from the scrap lumber pile to the north of the house, laid it on a frame of dead poplar trunks and notched it between two live trees. You lie there in high wind and feel the oceanic roll of poplar rhizomes under you and listen to the tick of leaves. Just below your back, grass fluxes with power. The path to this spot is marked with some Russian thistle tied to a tree with hay twine. I go there in the mornings at the end of May to pray the readings of the day, idle, hold in my mind my contemplatio of distraction. I read the

Phaedrus here over a couple of afternoons last summer, thinking about desire, puzzling over the good horse and the bad horse. One afternoon, I saw a deer feeding ten yards from me. I saw her a second before she noticed me; her bright body was an audacious nudity, a nakedness occupying the higher registers of the eye. It seemed an answer to something but I couldn't catch up to what that was. As the doe moved away — slowly so I wouldn't fully see it — I looked and looked.

I rest my back against one of the supporting aspens and stare at the woodhouse; to the southwest, clouds of a storm that swept around us earlier this morning. There's a sway of wild raspberries thirty yards long behind me, working along a hollow in the middle of the bush: it's born plump crops the last two years, given enough jars of jam to fill a shelf in the root cellar. A belt of saskatoons lies just beyond the raspberries — they're now barely out of blossom. A frost earlier this week killed the flowers on all the lower bushes; for another year there'll be berries only here and there and these likely to be largely seed. Poplar fluff blows and catches in the grass; spider webs whip between grass blades.

The complexity of the bush abashes me. There's something quicker than thinking in its casual and extreme variety. I could lie face down and stare at the few inches of ground before me: leaf mould, dead grass and new grass, chickweed in bloom, buffalo bean, roots, twigs, the moss with its green antlers at the base of aspens. The world, the world. I grasp some of it, but I'm just looking and feeling round the edges: what I'm staring at seems elsewhere, with itself. I can't be here; I can't go into this. I am away from it with my names for it; it is sequestered in its peculiar oddness. When I imagine myself leaving the names I call it and creeping toward it, every hard step I feel like giving up. I sometimes think of this giving up as etiquette and sometimes as exhaustion. Finally, however, there is no further going: the thing is fixed in the distance of its strangeness. The enervation I feel as I approach it, I am coming to suspect, is what knowing the things of the world feels like.

Plato says in the *Phaedrus* that when we love something or someone, we are reminded obscurely of a larger presence, absolute beauty, that feels most like home. Besotted, we set our foot on the rung of the ladder toward this terminus of our desire. Love is the beginning of advertence to higher things. The bush reminds me of nothing. Its formless, intentionless idiosyncrasy is adamant. The mind cannot lose the habit of anticipating a moment of recognition, the instant when it finds its bearings, but the bush repeatedly snubs this expectation.

*

The ambivalence of St. Augustine to the world is both epistemological and ascetical. In *De Doctrina Christiana,* he distinguishes between signs and things. Everything, he says, that gestures toward something else is first a thing, but not all things are signs. The members of the Trinity, for instance, unsurpassed and embracing everything, stand for nothing. Mundane objects, wood, stone, water, considered in a certain manner, are also simply things, mere phenomena, pointing nowhere. But these same things can also be seen as utterances from the hiddenness of God. Then the world is a divine writing, commanding attention because of the meaning it communicates, regard as a vehicle of transcendental intention, yet at the same time misleading if its numinous import is not kept paramount in mind. It takes a degree of skill to shape letters but that does not make them art. You properly treat a sentence by grasping the notion its speaker wishes to utter, not by admiring the consonants and vowels she assembles to do this. The world is to be simultaneously apprehended and ignored.

Augustine descries a further distinction among things themselves. Some things make us blessed and are to be enjoyed; others are to be used. "To enjoy something," he says, "is to cling to it with love for its own sake. To use something, however, is to employ it in obtaining that which you love, provided that it is worthy of love" (*De Doctrina Christiana,* Bk. I, IV, 4). The only things that can be properly enjoyed are those things of "our native country", God. All other things are of instrumental value — friendships, work, relaxations, the natural world. Used properly, each is a means of the soul finding its beatitude. But moral disaster results when things to be used are enjoyed. To understand the world as message-bearing is not only to know: it is to be pure.

One of the uses of the physical world, says Augustine, is a contemplative one: it provides insight into the supernatural cause of all that is, the invisible revealed by "things that are made". Nature is a book in which God bespeaks himself in a way, beyond the glimmer of surfaces. A contemplative study of it, for Augustine, also casts light on that other source of revelation, scripture. Here is where he finds close attention to the world most worthwhile. How are we to understand the figurative language of the Gospels, he asks, if we have no grasp of "the natures of animals, of stones, or plants"? The exhortation, for instance, to be wise as a serpent would mean little, says Augustine, if one had not observed that snakes when attacked will expose their bodies to protect their heads. This provides the unstated sense of the injunction: the believer should offer his body in martyrdom lest the faith be killed in him. The world commands our interest because, by hints, it helps us unravel the meanings of an infinite mind.

*

For Augustine, then, the world holds a version of God: it is what unique singularity looks like as a community of things. God is not limited by the world — cannot be exhausted by anything contained in time — but the world is essentially nothing other than divine speech. This conviction inspires but then troublingly undermines an attractive sort of attention to stones, grass, hills, lakes.

God lives somehow in such things. What does it mean you will see when you look at the world if you are convinced of this? You likely will consider it with the common attributes of divinity in mind as a map — or, perhaps, like a photograph of a stranger you have been asked to identify. You will hold the picture up to the real thing and look rapidly from one to the other. You will be sharp-eyed for flashes of power and beauty; you will note instances of providence in the way things appear to bend themselves to human utility. You will expect to find in things a version of immutability: the presence of an invariant order. Certain types of nature likely will claim the centre of your gaze, the ravishing, the mighty, mountain, waterfall. The alkaline lake will be something the eye passes over on its way to its rest elsewhere. Particular features within things — their goodness, for instance, what seems knowable or nameable in them, what seems like us — will stand out, announce themselves as definitive. A notion of the divine identity, then, assembled from religious art, say, bible stories or bits of Christian philosophy, will fashion seeing. Indeed, a mental picture sanctioned by dogmatic theology might replace the human gaze entirely with the act of interpretation.

Reverence toward the world can come with the belief that it is God-bearing. The wheatgrass stem bears the charge of the sacred. Here is sufficient impetus for a careful, courteous attentiveness to things that might be expected to end in an awful silence, the eye and feeling swallowed by root system, leaf shape, feather colour. But often some contemplative writers, Augustine and others, appear to pull away from such a gaze with troubling quickness, their inspection transmogrifying into rumination on essences or the web of being or bolting into the language of piety and praise. Their looking seems not wild and helpless enough, seems too nicely contained in understanding; it travels into the world only far enough to grasp the presence it anticipates; it appears to lack the terror of ecstasy. If you look hard enough at the world, past a region of comprehension surrounding things, you enter a vast unusualness that defeats you. You do not arrive at a name or a home. Look at a meadow long enough and your bearings vanish. The world seen deeply eludes all names; it is not like anything; it is not the sign of something else. It is itself. It is a towering strangeness. Even when it seems to expose itself by staring directly at you, you do not know it. To go into it is to leave the place where you live with your names for things and your sense of centrality. It is to go into a darkness and to feel small.

*

I take a walk in the back hills, late May, cold rain
falling. The land is thin and empty. Little thinking
rests on it; it is sparse even in this: who regards this
patch of waste? Now the bloom cones of
chokecherries candle in the bush. The deer, in tight
thickets, are giving birth these weeks under a moon
building to full. The nighthawks are back; Bonaparte
gulls wobble over aspen stands and hollows. The
grass, under the rain, is a hefty shove, is massive yet
intricate, calming and fuddling the eye as glossolalia
might the ear.

A fire went through here six years ago, spreading
from the railway tracks to the west and charring a half
mile belt of poplar; new trees have grown in and now,
this spring, are my height. A fireguard ploughed at the
time of the blaze has also grown in, but its grasses,
brome and crested wheat, are different than the older
prairie on either side of the cut, less blue and spiked.
The land is sand, parts of it blown into dunes, and
covered lightly in low bush, cacti and fescue. This is
the delta of a glacial river. It's good country for game;
aboriginal kill sites lie everywhere on it, the bones of
bison lying in places just a few feet under the scrawny
topsoil. The sandy uselessness of the hills and flats has
saved them from the cultivation that goes on all
around.

Two years ago, I was walking the fireguard and had
just crested a small rise when a coyote moved from the
bush, trotted a few yards ahead and turned to look at
me. Plato says the goal of human eros is to return.
Return to what? The Good, says Plato. But there is

another story of the return that claims the place we wish to go back to is the world, the world restored to its earliest unions, the Garden, the world with human consciousness finally nested in it. The coyote's look seemed a light glimpsed in a forest on a windy night: that's where I've been heading. But I had no idea what lay there or if, in any sense, I was awaited.

There is a region of unknowability in the coyote and its look, in the fervid idiosyncrasy of grass, lying behind the names we call it, where the mind is humiliated. The difference in things woos names from us: we wish to draw what we see toward us. The naming accelerates; it becomes praise, a form of possession that seems like release. But praising is an assertion of language that erases language. One epithet sings the thing wholly and sunders all other names. At the end of the tongue that has sung its songs is a sheer drop into what-one-knows-not. All things in their breathtaking otherness have nothing to do with us, but our deepest desire insists on bending us toward them, stripping us from ourselves, from language, from a feeling of being masters in our own house. Long seeing casts us out of doors and impoverishes. We go into the strange terrain of what the grass is in itself, into that large night, and lie down, waiting.

49

*

The experience of looking hard at things which is the contemplation of the world undermines the psychological preconditions of any doctrinal idealism. How dare you assert the identity of a thing with something else when your gaze tells you that it is beyond all naming? Reverent attention reveals a thing's indifferent oddness before which you feel small. Your engulfment by the object in contemplation makes the claims of idealism seem like presumption; the self-effacement of contemplation injures such presumption. The courtesy toward the thing that contemplation engenders causes you to flinch from such discountings of its particularity in favour of an "essence". All you can do is look and look, momentumed by your apokatastatic eros toward the thing, but unable to comprehend it in its vast individuality. You can bed down with things; you can come alongside them and attend.

To look at the world with awe is to have intellect humbled by the borderless expanse of specific things, so that the contemplative cannot name what dwells in this poplar, this oatgrass head, or, even, if either is the residence of any informing presence. The extent of the singular thing merely invites the contemplative look to persist, to travel on, and the look, if it is honest, if it reserves nothing of itself from awe, if it keeps nothing of itself chaste, will not come to rest in conviction, but *will* move on, wondering, probing deeper into things. Here the mind will experience the unmitigated separateness of the coyote and the hill as loneliness and truth. The look goes on, refusing to suppress any of the raggedness of individuality.

Eros eventually comes to sorrow. The appetite to understand and become whole in the union of the self with what it knows vaults you into the world and the more graceful your knowledge of the world is the further away the world seems. One of the ends of noesis is etiquette: letting what you sufficiently esteem to want to know remain itself. The point is not to counter one ontology with another, materialism, for instance, for idealism: each grasps in a way that skews the object. The point is to not allow ontological loyalties to shape seeing. Credo ut intelligam: yes, but what one holds to be true can also shrink what one knows, pulling it toward unexamined pictures within itself. Many things cause one to regard the world with appetite, fideistic certitude, loneliness, despair, but these must be suspended once they have managed to turn us toward what we most elementally love or they will lead us to a seeing that employs the world merely as raw material for human images of the world.

The eros to return to the world leads you to a *51* thinning of self. You are forced to set aside what you take knowing to be; you are forced to discount what your imagination suggests union is, what it hints return shall be. You must do this because the eros by which you return to the world hurtles past all ways you thought this might unfold deeper into the lonely strangeness around things that are receding as you love them more. Finally, this peregrinatio into the desert of what things are in their distance comes to feel less like choosing than drift, the self lightly magneted by the thing. Contemplation of nature places you far from the noetic mainstream where names are near at hand and definitions possible with effort; it makes you marginal, putting you in the company of things never properly seen. You lie down with what is ignored. The poplar and the hill back away into their peculiar identities as the eros to know them thrusts you forward; the one thing that remains intimate and clear is your own desire. You are beyond the gravity of the mind's propriety and caught in the gravity of things. Consciousness becomes feral.

Sorrow;

The

River

— South Saskatchewan River —

It is in the evening that one breaks up,
at sunset.
Then it is that one abandons everything.

Mind takes down its tents of spider web,
and heart forgets why it felt anxious.
The desert wanderer abandons his campsite,
which will soon be obliterated by sand,
and continues on his journey in the stillness of night,
guided by mysterious stars.

      - from *Evening Land*, Pär Lagerkvist

Dark ice rolls and drifts on the river, form without
intention; sandbars blur through the motion. Dark
river, burly aimlessness, gathering and losing itself,
darkening in mid-November. Its pale banks are clay,
poplar: the sand of the thin beaches has begun to
freeze, gull feathers and smooth sticks trapped inside;
where the sand is dented with hoof prints or is wind-
worked, dips of early snow hold out against melting in
the afternoons. The last geese are on the river, some
big mallards from further north. They cluster at the
willow-lit island at dusk — mostly geese.

The river can't be known because it is an unlikeness: you can guess but in guessing here the truest guess is the most deferential, wobbling with equivocation, the one whose assertion permits itself to be dismantled even while it is being made. The one who makes it knows that what is being said may appear to suffice, but that whatever the river is it is such and such in so utterly a distant way that the names of the qualities assigned it can't possibly go deep. The names expose the namer more than they limn what's caught the eye. The act of naming, too, seems an encasement and the confidence of this feels wrong; it would seem even comic if such presumptions weren't so dangerous. The best names are wadded about with apology; they duck their heads because they are abashed. They are abashed because naming is what humans do and believing that names are co-terminous with essences is an error humans typically make: but none of this has to do with the river, none of this knows the river, is close to the river, except perhaps whatever loneliness and beguilement quickened the naming.

Even if the river were me, I couldn't know it: think of Augustine's consternation before the indeterminate complexity of his own much-considered soul in the *Confessions*.

The river is a dark thing and it is infinite.

*

When Gregory of Nazianzen became bishop of the small orthodox community in the imperial capital of Constantinople in 379, Arians had held power in that see for many years: they had the favour of the emperor Valens, his wife; most of the people followed this line of thinking. Eunomius, bishop of Cyzicus, prolific and astute, stood tall among the disputatious enthusiasts of the heterodox community; he stirred and shaped the theological talk in the circles of the enlightened; his *Liber Apologeticus* not only affirmed the mind's ability to plumb the depths of God, but also denied the divinity of the Son. This denial was premised on a confidence that the clarity of names, arrived at by effort of logic, revealed essence. Nazianzen began his episcopal ministry with a brace of homilies in the small chapel of Anastasia against both Eunomian doctrinal claims and methodology, attacking first the Arians' epistemological self-assurance. Gregory called Eunomian speculations "too generous", yet said they impoverished what they sought to illuminate.

Eunomius insisted that the whole of God could be examined fully by "clear and unadulterated reasoning" and be expressed exhaustively in language (*Liber Apologeticus,* 20). This conviction concerning the sufficiency of reason and language rested on the belief that distinctions in logic had ontological significance. Something separable in mind would be autonomous in reality: if one thing has two names, it had parts or had been carelessly conflated with something else. A quality adumbrated by reason, for Eunomius, pointed to a distinct essence: thus his Arianism: if God the Father were unbegotten, as the Nicene Creed (325 A.D.) said he was, he could not be the same as the Son, whom the same creed declared to be begotten. Since God could not be imagined as having parts, the Son, Eunomius claimed, distinguishable in his begottenness, possessed a different essence, was not God. Or again: the mind assigns a quality to a thing — "pre-eminence" in the case of the first person of the Trinity — because surely such a property is possessed by the investigated subject: such superiority cannot be shared: the Son, once more, was not God. The divine world is considered speech reified.

Eunomius resembles Descartes in the hegemony he offers reason; like Descartes, as well, his efforts to comprehend tend to shrink what they seek to know. Eunomians, Gregory complained, were prepared to make "our great mystery" a "thing of little moment" in order that it be lit by reason. Descartes equally pared what he sought to elucidate, the world, God, himself, of whatever reason could not utter — specificity in the case of the world, the ambiguous fact of the thing as the senses knew it, thereby coming to a physical reality of mere extension, conformable to the language of mathematics and geometry. A particular theology lies beneath Eunomian epistemic confidence: God used names for things to draw them into existence, hawthorne berry, crested wheat, before the creation of human beings, so these names are "older than those who use them" (*An Apology for the Apology,* Bk. II, ii, 303.1-6). It is proper to the dignity of creation, the greatness of the creator, that these names are a fitting bestowal, true mirroring of natures in speech. God cannot act out of caprice without self-contradiction; the names are not arbitrary. Even after the office of naming fell to humans, appellations were not plucked from the air, but natures were uttered: what these words, all unfallen, words undergirded by meticulous thought, meant were what things were — "the real meanings are determined on the basis of underlying objects" (*An Apology,* Bk. II, v. 368.6-18). For Descartes as well it was impossible to believe that God would have made a world not reducible to reason. God, after all, had a particular sympathy for what struck the mind with clarity and distinctness: on this alone he would not allow deception to contaminate the mind of the careful thinker.

*

The river is dark, willows along it reddening as winter begins; deer trails curve down to the water through heavily grassed clay bluffs: with a little snow these hold the light well into evening. The river, black amnesia, dragon-current, moves through Saskatoon; it moves past a chemical plant, an aboriginal culture centre, then into wolf willow and snowberry bush. Crowsnest, Old Man, St. Mary's, Bow, Red Deer: each of these rivers come into it; it moves through cottonwood groves, badlands, empty country; it's passed through turbines at Outlook; maps show it feeding into swampy lands in northern Manitoba; somehow it finds its way to Lake Winnipeg. It is black, indifferent; it sidles away from human utterance. It is too far out in the unbidden world to reach. To desire it is to be humiliated.

59

The river is a sleep and a grazing; it is the genius of inertia; its momentum is a darkness, the heavy, shy river, fat, blind river, the great world, moving through grass. The river is elm-crooked, eccentric, gathered-into-itself; it is sloppy with sandbars, oxbows, sudden deep bits; no one swims in it because its currents are dangerous, no motorboats on it for any long stretch because of the pillowing sand, because of dead trees stranded in the flow. The river is distance, it is manyness, it is incalculability. This is not a naming but a praising, a sway in the tongue. This is also a lament sung by thinking.

*

The impulse to clarity in both Eunomius and Descartes issues in reductionism: what judgement affirms is not a knowledge of a subject but a transformation of it. There is nothing yielding in Cartesian or Eunomian comprehension, no deference, no accommodation in the reception of the object of knowledge: it is a rigour that truncates that to which it turns. God is appealed to in both systems to act as a guarantor of what the mind knows clearly: Descartes, in his *Meditations on First Philosophy,* finds no way from the solipsism of the cogito until he assures himself that God both exists and is not a deceiver, will not permit him, that is, to be misled on things that strike him as indubitably clear. God guarantees with both Eunomius and Descartes the veracity of what one knows, not only by making evident through scripture and the apparent order of the world a preference for simple geometric symmetries in creating and for the accuracy of names, but also by directly aiding the thinker through cognitive assurance: your convictions, insofar as they are the product of reflection untouched by the senses or the credulity of awe, are sequestered from error. Cognitive certitude underwritten by divine ministration: here the distortion of the senses, the distortion of credulous wonder, hold no sway. The ambition of this certitude is the acquisition of command, the assurance of one's salvation through noesis for the Arians, the transformation, in Descartes' case, of human knowers from fruitless speculators to "masters and possessors of nature" (*Discourse on Method,* Part 6, 62). There are gnostic elements in both men; with both, there is a shying before the wilderness of indeterminacy. The result in Eunomian theology, as Gregory remarked, is a God amputated of mystery; in Cartesian physics, the world is shrunk to dimension and motion.

*

The ice-pintoed river, the river's dark eye, the river's
loneliness, its darkness, unlikeness, distance: the river
flows. It moves through the buckskin, tufted land,
between taupe bluffs, over sand bars, around caught
white-dead trees, around islands of willows and
rabbits. Its cruising ice, the masses of ice, split on the
wedges of bridge supports built years ago by now
dead concrete-men; the masses heave into one
another; the one following the pile of ice now being
split passes under it. All this is both nothing and more
than can be said.

*

Everything exceeds its name: insofar as the named
world is co-terminous with the finite world,
everything is infinite. The weight of everything, its
home, where it is itself, lies beyond naming, lives
outside the range of calculation, is not, if to be is to
possess a name. The mysterium of the physical world
is a theophany of what is not there, that is beyond the
calibrations that erect "thereness". Thus, as John
Scotus Eriugena says, "no substance or essence of any
creation, whether visible or invisible, can be
comprehended by the intellect or by reason as to what
it is" (*Periphyseon,* 443B). Thus, in their largeness,
complexity, dissimilarity, things are properly
addressed by awe, by gratitude for the generosity of
their proximity; names whose prelude is awe are
tentative, are acquiescent to their own withdrawal:
they possess courtesy and because this courtesy, this

softness, this amenability to alteration, reversal, is the residue in language of wonder, these names are true, not in the sense that they map a thing, but that they possess an apt decorum; they do not lie; they do not presume. The river that is registered in the inchoate, leaping delight of the senses is an absence in reason, a silence in language, a silence even within the excess of ecstatic speech. At best the chaotic river, alive in the senses briefly, is discountable, has no standing in definition; before the severity of Cartesian doubt, it does not exist.

How does one address what falls outside reason's caricatures, that eludes language's efforts to circumscribe, that has no being if being is equal to comprehensibility, espiability of form? Here naming may be nothing more than ovation, or a mark of the assertions and reversals of apophasis, or a slight domestication of being in which we participate in what is beyond us, enjoy a brief contiguity with that uncontainability, like feeding birds in winter.

There is praise and then there is sorrow.

*

The problem with Eunomian speculation on the divinity, Gregory told his congregation, is that it isn't touched by virtue; he must "speak against those who pride themselves on their eloquence", he says: it is not the vanity of mere flair that concerns him or even sophistry: a more malign assurance operates here: this is speech, underwritten by a hubris of reason, that transmogrifies what it utters, and, thus, subsequently, misshapes those who hear it, the piety they erect, the world — present and supernatural — this piety shapes. There is something too troublingly assured in

Eunomian eristics — an intolerable evil Gregory calls
it — too swashbuckling, yet painstaking: an alteration
is being wrought that malforms the nature of things.
"Not to everyone," he says, "does it belong to
philosophize about God; not to everyone — the
subject is not so cheap and low — and, I will add, not
before every audience, not at all times, nor on all
points; but on certain occasions and before certain
persons and within certain limits." Only those "who
have been previously purified in soul and body, or at   *63*
the very least are being purified" may so speculate.
"For the impure to touch the pure is . . . not safe . . ."
(*Theological Orations,* I, 3).

If there is no virtue, there is no comprehension:
indeed, comprehension *is* virtue, a stance that receives
the whole thing awkwardly, blindly, with gratitude,
without being able to report this reception, a stance
composed of borderless awe and human powers
thinned by compunction, these powers relieved of
presumption. Gregory's embargo on the hegemonous
exercise of reason, his delimitation of its ambition, is
not obfuscation but advertence to the unspeakable
reaches of things, a noting of the modesty of capacity
that is the rudiment of decorum. And it is this
decorum, fully developed, which is knowledge: it is
also relationship, protean, never coming to term. And
what makes one pure? The sorrow of knowing one is
separated from what one would know in its
unmitigated unlikeness, the sorrow, for Gregory, of
knowing that the dissimilarity of God makes the eros
to know God unsatisfiable, the sorrow of knowing that
one is hopelessly outside the paradise that would exist
if one lived in the world as if it were home, of
knowing this while not being relieved of the desire to
so live. Not obfuscation: "For we ought to think of

God even more than we draw breath; and if the expression is permissible, we ought to do nothing else" and so be "molded to purity" (*Theological Orations,* I, 5). But "geometry is out of place in mourning".

*

The river is dark: it is a bone no more than a month out of the body, greasy, furred with dirt. Tears are the far promontory of knowledge; the river is just as far off on its own: two darknesses, two momentums in which there is no hesitation, no looking back, they simply head where they are going; this is not singlemindedness, but feeling the weight of all that has happened at one's back, the uninterest in, the incapacity for, negotiation in this weight. With tears, what carries you along is what you will do, but it's not human, perhaps not humane. Yet it is delectable.

*

The Syrian word for monk, the person given without remainder to contemplation, is the name for those honoured in the second beatitude: blessed are those who mourn. Sorrow is the way back, sorrow the return. It is the telos that the eros to know God, the eros to recover lost salvation, comes to, said the desert monks: it is the state to which the desire to live in the world as if it were home, to know the blond river as at least as unestranged as oneself, comes. The river is dark; it is infinite: penthos approaches it; sorrow delivers one awkwardly, unexpectedly, uncertainly to it. Inquiry into things, the river, grass, comes to courtesy — and courtesy without awe is confected and awe without compunction is confected — or it lies.

Sorrow is the telos of contemplation, the shape, as well, that reason would assume at the edge of its range if it were honest, but it is not the sadness that, full grown, is despair. This is a deposit of acedia, penthos' dark counterfeit, like unbroken, wheedling, multiform discontent, like avidity for distraction, a disfiguring of interiority, softening of the singlemindedness contemplation urges, wrought, the old monks said, by the passions. Its cure was one's cell that would teach one everything: the rigour of that place checked any slide into acedia's dolour, the temptation to flee the humiliation of one's understanding, and one's appetite to circumscribe, through melancholy. "The spirit of sadness drives away tears," warns Evagrius Ponticus, "the spirit of sadness ruins prayer." Penthos is vivifying, a maintaining of the pitch of desire; it is a ravishing: acedia's depression enervates; it is wilful and petulant: tears and stability, keeping to where one is, correct the malign drift.

Sorrow is the alteration of self before extreme dissimilarity; it is admission of the unlikeness of what one cranes toward and one's exclusion from its beauty, its community, and thus is what knowledge of the thing's uncontainability feels like; sorrow is what fashions courtesy, work of reverence, toward what one would know utterly. It is what makes it possible for us to live with what we would know, a renunciation drawing us near. Sorrow disarms the passions so that other life may live contiguous with human consciousness safely. Within this sorrow is gratitude for the augmentation of the oddity of what one wishes to comprehend but cannot. You are struck by the generosity of things being what they are; you are enlarged by this generosity. But sorrow is not wooed by such generosity; advertence to the possibility of generosity comes through penthos. And penthos appears suddenly, says John Chrysostom, through a blow of quick remorse, a smart visitation: one is "nailed", he says, to this sorrow by a stroke of horror in which you are arrested by the wrongness of how you proceed. He calls this experience catanyxis. The confidence of reason, its intentness in Descartes on the reduction of the human person to mental acts issuing in indubitable knowledge, the reshaping of things so that the world is no larger than the human capacity for mathematical clarity, its conviction in Eunomius that it left no residue when it named, reason's hegemonous grandeur, proofs it against such an altering shock, penthos' antechamber.

"Tears falling on a corpse cannot restore it, but if they fall on a soul they will bring it back to life." Penthos, says St. Ephrem, quickens one to note one's manufactured apartness — one's distance, he said, from paradise, one's separation from God, the distortion of the imago Dei. Thus, penthos establishes right relationship: further, tears are, in a primitive sense, political, a social labour; they are, says Gregory of Nazianzen, "the purification of the world".

*

Late January now; the river is tight with ice; in places the green-brown flow has smoothed the ice above it thinner. At Cranberry Flats, snow humps over the ice cover; fox and coyote tracks wave toward the willow and cottonwood island. The river is a cave, a hard domicile of unlikeness, its dissimilarity a cell where you can station yourself and be brought to a small courtesy by the resolute unknowability of something beautiful and far. It's unexpected that the impulse to know may come to sorrow, that all desire may come here, that this transformation of self in tears is where knowledge was headed by inclination all along, to a decorum that remains erotic.

The bank grass in snow, brome grass, clatters; the river is a white sweep; willow tips are pale orange; the dogwood is helplessly red.

THERE
IS NO
Presence

— The Quill Lakes —

The northwest shore of Little Quill Lake, on the low
ridge separating it from Mud Lake, in falling light: the
grass is long-legged and naked. You walk in this grass;
you are poor walking here. Tundra swans are blazing
on the water; their whiteness makes them leap in the
eye. Distance rolls over the fierce incalculability of the
grass; there are salt flats just a little south, then the
thick poplar bush of the Touchwood Hills, then creeks,
range land, stubble, big rivers, south, south. The birds,
quiet on the lake or in big, deflated grey-blue clouds
on the fields, eating spilled grain, are pulling a single
momentum into themselves. No sound but the flap of
clothes in the push of the wind. Snow geese lift in far,
gangly bunches, nervous under the circle of a bald
eagle; you see this through the shiver lines of distance,
and it is like hearing slow, floating music in a plugged
ear.

I think: let me be found here, after four winters,
down by the water, drinking with the deer. I imagine
myself whiter, thin, more convinced and simple,
angled away, alert, a far thing. Or I imagine myself
with the breast of the grass in my mouth, taking in its
clay-ey milk, the gold body I keep in my body,
emotion's body, growing dark hair along its shoulder

blades as I suck. I want to go back; I want to go away. This means leaving the wealth of my name. This is terrifying, but it is not renunciation; it is eros playing itself out. Desire impoverishes; desire is a thinning, but this is because untruncated delight is apokatastatic; its telos is true home, the community of all things, and one arrives there, if at all, less. Desire and its transmogrifications, shame and penthos, are sustenance enough for the way back; plain delight knows the way.

Abba James told the story of an elder in the Egyptian desert whose neighbour was a child living in solitude. The elder heard the boy praying one day for whatever it was he needed to live in peace with the animals: a hyena was feeding its brood nearby, "and the child slipped himself under and began nursing with them." Desire dreams peculiar fates; it is intimate and outlandish; at full stretch, it arrives at strange satisfactions that come into view only partly along the way that desire picks out, desire's meanderings to these seemingly a matter of war, loss and the disappointment of others.

Abba Macarius told another story: one day, he felt urged to go to a part of the desert that few visited, where he found a lake with a small island in it; here the animals came in the evenings. "In the midst of these animals, I saw two naked men. They said, 'It is God who has made this way of life for us. We do not freeze in the winter and the summer does us no harm.'" Desire's sense of aptness is unnerving.

The lake is flat and blinding. There are coyote here, cougar, lynx; four years ago, not far from this place, I saw a jack-rabbit that stood a little higher than my waist. We eyed one another a long minute across dock and horsetail. All that afternoon, I walked alkaline flats looking, looking, all the light in me, the light of desire, the light of intelligence, the light of seeing, seemed the proboscis of a primitive animal. Far away, birds rose, then dropped again into the yellow grass.

Intense seeing delivers you to poverty. You look, your seeing an approach, the offer of an agreement between you and what has drawn your attention, but what you see is unmoved by your approach, untouched by the look, indifferently far, unlike, unaccommodating. To look with appetite is to have the ambitions of the look mortified. If you desire the grass because, finally, the beauty of the grass has arrested you, you are undermined while beguiled. The reach of the grass, the muscularity of its multiplicity, is beyond you; you are made small. But if you come to be innocent, the old desert stories imply, if you set aside confidence in your capacity, if you release your weight into the graceful engine of something other than your will, you may find yourself coming alongside things. If you follow desire into its alarming frontiers. If desire begins to act as an ascetic power, an emptying force at odds with the aplomb of the self, then, say the stories, you may arrive at a place where you feel yourself brushed by the sides of milling animals, in late daylight beside a cold lake, a little ice on the water, a moon coming up over grass.

*

Simone Weil remarked in *Gravity and Grace* that astronomy and chemistry represented degradations of the attention that astrology and alchemy could muster. A further degradation happens, she said, when alchemy and astrology become forms of magic. The precision of observation, description and prediction chemistry and astronomy can achieve, while making the world seem clearer, represent a fading of human engagement with the world. Further, the requirements of this precision — its positing of a version that fits with its capacity and with its ambition to speak with utter clarity — represents a remodelling of the world that prejudices human enthralment with it. Galileo's primary qualities and Descartes' properties of extension and motion are not capable of arousing awe and tenderness.

Regard is related to morality; a degradation of regard issues in a diminution of courtesy: once a thing is not attended at all in its unyielding distance, it becomes a caricature and, then, is a part of the self, over which the self has absolute powers. No decorum need be exercised before such a diminished thing. Behaviour toward it will improve only once a way has been found to recall a thing's beauty. Such a remembrance may have no explanatory usefulness but can still play the role of a moral heuristic. For moral reasons, a new depiction of the world is required, though this may not result in a clearer grasp of the world, nor in more muscular predictive powers concerning it.

Plato distinguishes between two types of image-making, "two species of mimetics", in the *Sophist:* the phantastic and the eikastic arts. Phantastic endeavour is the confection of apparition, a distorted image the intent of which is enchantment, its enervation, the game of the sophist. Eikastic image making aims to "give back simply the true proportions of the beautiful things" (236a). You see Socrates constructing such images in his description of the beautiful city in the *Republic* and in the soul's chariot ascent in the

Phaedrus; by such images, he wants to stir in Glaucon and Phaedrus a desire for the good, an appetite for real beauty. The beauty of the image of the beauty beyond being will shape the soul: virtue will result, one of the effects of this ravishment.

*

There is a singing in things. Or you can call it a sleep. Its beauty is a kind of loyalty, an upholding, a patriotism for something that does not seem to exist. Though immense, it is frail. This shining tone in things vanishes to be replaced by sentiment and ownership as soon as any sort of relationship with it is assumed. I want this thing and this wanting will make me poor.

*

John Scotus Eriugena was the West's first translator of the pseudo-Dionysius the Areopagite. He was attached to the court of Charles the Bald, a peregrinator from Ireland who arrived in France in 848. He worked as a teacher of the liberal arts; between 862 and 866, he wrote his mammoth work *Periphyseon, The Division of Nature.*

The monism of this work is Dionysian but more carefully sketched in than the monism of *The Divine Names.* For pseudo-Dionysius, being is divine ekstasis; for Eriugena, too, natura designated the created world but also that which creates it; all things, for Eriugena, are theophanies; "God is created in the creature" (678 c). Everything, then, is at once nature and grace; nothing is that does not participate in super-essential goodness: such participation is both subsistence and teleology. The movement from higher to lower essences is river-like, he says, and, except in broad metaphoric adumbration, unspeakable: "So the Divine Goodness and Essence and Life and Wisdom and everything which is in the source of all things first flow down into the primordial causes, then through the primordial causes they descend in an ineffable way through the orders of the universe that accommodate them, flowing forth continuously, through the higher to the lower; and return back again to their source through the most secret channels of nature by a most hidden course" (632c). The world, low hills, grass, clay banks of rivers, geese, rivers flowing east, late afternoon light, is a single thing, is divinity ambling out of itself, divinity plotting a return to a point of immutable undifferentiation. The "inexhausted diffusion from [the Divinity] in Itself back to Itself, is the cause of all things, indeed *is* all things" (632d).

But the world, though full of God, God the stone in the stone, the world thus full, is not the exhaustion of God, says Eriugena: things are speech, but the mind exposed by language remains invisible; "it is both silent and cries out" (633c). What God is in this divine superessentiality, Eriugena says, can't be said — it is "nothing", all that is beyond intelligence — but things themselves are also beyond knowing. Things are both eternal and made; of their essential nature, their eternal nature, you can say only that they are but not what they are (655c-d); the "more secretly" each thing is understood, "the closer it is seen to approach the divine brilliance" (681b).

The oddness of this sort of speech aside — its unlikeness to the explanatory speech of the last four hundred years — there are some difficulties with Eriugena's cosmological formulation. If things are essentially divine, what of their accidents, their colours, their shapeliness, their alterations — *this* grass stalk moving in the wind? These seem too full of mutability to have a divine source; they seem not to stand still for thinking, are murky with change. How much of all is divine? Another problem: if things are divine in their essences, and perhaps as well in their accidents, they must be somehow infinite: how are they, then, to be known? How are their names legitimate?

The problem of the status of accidents is related, I think, to the problem of naming. If God is only the essence of things and not their accidents, things are unnamable, infinite and eternal only essentially, but in their accidents they may be named, yet are less astoundingly noteworthy. But Eriugena has said that God is all that is: therefore, if accidents are, they too must be God: thus all things are essentially, and in their accidents, more than their names by the measure of God. The *Periphyseon* itself seems of two minds concerning accidents, the world as the senses dote on it. In one place, Eriugena claims that only forms and species are theophanies, but elsewhere he states that divine essence includes a thing's quantity "and its quality and the bond between all things and its position and habit and place and time and action and passion and everything whatsoever that can be understood by whatsoever intellect in every creature and about every creature" (681d-682a).

If everything about a thing is divine, the thing cannot be uttered in total truth. It is its name but more than its name. It merits a multitude of names; it is approached best by praise, a form of naming which has given up the project of identification in a sort of drunkenness, a form of naming which is unthinkable without wonder, that shining and disarmed step toward the world. The stutter of apophasis, the naming which is always undoing itself while remaining erotically momentumed to what woos the names, is the speech of wonder. It can't utter truth, but it expresses and helps shape a stance which is apt; it is itself a mark of graceful relationship.

But the matter of apophatic speech and things can be taken further. One wishes to groom Eriugena's cosmology as an image to beckon virtue and so will say: there is presence. But a higher expression of this is to say there is no presence, a denial that holds, as something residual, the smell of the affirmation, yet unbendingly resists all images and anticipations — of conversation, community, of forgiveness from the world — that the affirmation of presence engendered. All images of the divine in things must be expunged lest another reductionism, another elimination of the thing, a pious one now, be wrought. At the same time, the regard for the thing that the initial assertion of presence set in place must be maintained. There is presence, there is no presence, yes, but the negation is higher. The helplessness such speech creates is part of the poverty which might gain you admission to the silent company of the grass.

*

I want to go back. It seems ludicrous to want this. Want to bed down beside things. I don't want to be alone in that part of me that wants some familial relation with the grass. I want to be married there, home, quiet, looking around. I want to go back. Maybe it's just that I want to be heard as matter, heard as animal, want to be heard in this broad a way, and want the rest that such recognition would spread along the whole muscle of self. Bush land, hump land, slow, turned away, birds lifting and falling, the sleep of randomness. I am lonely for where I am, miss a bedding down with things, a gathering at the water. The expulsion from Eden, Aristophanes' tale in the *Symposium,* reports the breadth and pang of such feelings of deprival.

But you can't power yourself there, can't wrestle into yourself the simplicity you might imagine the task of return requires. The confection of a virtuous stupidity seems like more of the narcissism one would like to leave behind. It's better if you bend to the beauty of things, unmanaged, untranslatable beauty, then see what virtue the beauty brings. Proximity will never be effortless: here human beings limp. There will always be the envelope of valuing and doing which self-consciousness casts up.

Esteem for the world woos decorum, a softness, an indirectness of approach. It provokes gratitude; you note the generosity of things, the generosity of things being nothing other than what they are. Esteem lays open the possibility of receiving what the world might offer if it weren't simply the object of management. I'll go down to the river, wolf-coloured hunch of water; I'll go down to the lake. I like the poverty of the river, the beauty of this poverty. Here's an absence to aspire to. It is "widowed", "orphaned" as I would like to be, the slimness to which desire painfully, beneficently delivers you. I'll go down to the river as a discipline, to the wolf-coloured hump of water. This is love and admiration, the courting of ascesis, the sweet inkling of home-coming in the divesting of what feels most home-like: the centrality of oneself.

But there is no home and there is no arrival. This is

always so, even far along in the erotic enterprise. To
imagine there are is to still calculate, to still colonize
what is with fantasy and, thus, to abandon the genius
of desire.

*

Metaphor does not tell the truth. All poets are liars: the
river is a sleep and a grazing; it is dragon muscle; it is
shut-mouthed eloquence. Socrates, assembling images
to evoke the beautiful and the good, lies: the beautiful
city never was or will be, the city that is the soul
written in letters large enough for Socrates and
Glaucon to read. "Socrates does injustice, and is
meddlesome, by investigating the things under the
earth and the heavenly things and by making the
weaker speech the stronger and by teaching others
these same things" (*Apology*, 19b-c). Metaphor in the
form of the eikastic image may give priority to the
speech weak in clarity. Eriugena's monism can seem
at least far-fetched; at worse, it may appear
obscurantist, the suppression of accurate knowledge.

Metaphor does not tell the truth, but it can make
truthful promises. With Socrates' plausible tales, the
invitation is made: act as if this were so and you will
become liberal, humane, good. If you allow the beauty
that I have limpingly hinted at to lure your desire,
your eudaemonic craving will be satisfied. The world
may be misspoken in the Socratic image, yet the soul
is well led, well shaped.

What is human longing like? It's as if we had
existed before and in this previous existence had
followed the gods along a steep path until we stood
with them upon the back of the universe and saw
things "beyond the skies" of such beauty that none can

sing them. And it's as if we wish to return to this matchless sight; this is what the reach of desire feels like (*Phaedrus,* 247b). Only a god can render the soul as it is; we however can touch what is humanly unspeakable by noting what it resembles (246a). The world is as if God were the world; it is *that* beautiful, ordered, provident, perduring. Or at least this is how it seems when human beings think of their desire for it. Eriugena over-speaks the physical world and renders with accuracy the only satisfactory relationship between human interiority and what is.

Cartesian philosophy has a tin ear for such utterance. This is a willed disability: part of the purity the asceticism of Cartesian method sets out to achieve is just this inability to be drawn by such speech.

*

Desire comes to sorrow because it cannot have what it wants in the way it has come to anticipate appropriation; this sorrow can crimp the self into a citizen of the polis of all things; it may shape one to come alongside the grass, to bed down with things. The sorrow desire arrives at, penthos, said the old monks, was the goal of the contemplative life. They insisted though that this was not despair, which they said was a symptom of acedia, the condition you fell into if after entering the desert you turned away from solitude. The difference between penthos and despair is that the latter entertains all sorts of anticipations yet is disappointed in each, while the other refuses all images anticipation suggests to it, yet remains erotic, reaching, within this refusal. Despair is the abandonment of desire. Here is grievance, a sense of injustice, calculations for redress, hopelessness.

Penthos has no hope either, but this absence isn't crushing loss; it is poverty. Revelation aside, penthos has nothing other than the momentum and queer vector of eros, the stripping of this.

*

White grass showing through snow, poplars ghosting up from a dip, late light, the heavy, shallow lake — land off on its own, unsubsidized by human seeing: Eriugena is erotically right: something entices that intelligence doesn't know. But if the nose of desire has ascertained something that is endless, dark, this thing is mistreated by names though many names may seem its due. It must be approached apophatically: there is presence, but since this is likely to conjure reductive images: there is no presence. The negation is not skepticism but a stride toward what cannot be spoken, even can't be caught by flimsy images of ethereality. In the erasure of names, while the press of naming continues, eros moves its blind hand on the unknowable thing, not to discern shape but to achieve a restless, shifting contiguity, to accomplish a touch. Desire is an animal brushing against other animals as they move down to the water.

EPEKTASIS;

UNDER THE

INSTRUCTION OF

Things

— Saskatoon —

For Don McKay & Jan Zwicky

Summer river, jewelled variety; fat, flirtatious, yet
oblique, bank grasses, a green, vegetable mist over the
evening river. Poverty is the clearing in which the
world strides toward you: lose and the wheat is closer.
You cannot craft this accommodating absence, of
course: the conviction that a proximity to the world
can be erected is the error which in its most naïve
form is sentimentality, the production of a simulacrum
of the world that thrusts the world away in favour of
the self in lurid delusion. But what makes this home-
offering absence can be undergone; it can be visited
on you. Horror, humiliation, grief, regret, upending
ravishment can unfold into a capacity that feels like a
giving up, the collapse of competence, can become a
withdrawal, providing room where things may
manifest themselves with the least possible
qualification, a place where all things can slowly open
their eyes, as Wu-men Hui-k'ai (1183-1260) said.
Humiliation, grief, regret can alter into beauty and
kinship: poverty in us is like the forgottenness in grass
which is the furthest tip of its beauty; it may place us
in the family of grass. Lose and the wheat is closer.
   The desert, in monasticism, is not the theatre of

self-abnegation, but is an erotic place. It was not ambitioned into being by the august will — such a project seems ludicrous, fated and dangerous to others — but desire found it, a discovery stumbled on against all odds, an unlikely home along the way. Loss is an intermediate end of desire, an out-of-range lure that tugs unsettlingly on the vector of sensible intent; the desert guards the things that are good for desire. Shame can be felt here, compunction; here one can fit the whole self into the momentum of erotic singlemindedness; you are small enough for this. So it's a home for eros and a benefactor feeding it good things. Remain in your cell and it will teach you everything, said the Egyptian monks. "The necessity for a reward, the need to receive the equivalent of what we give. But if, doing violence to this necessity, we leave a vacuum, as it were a suction of air is produced and a supernatural reward results," said Simone Weil (*Gravity and Grace,* 10). Lose and the garden may configure around you.

*

Look around: there's enough to regret. Stand back from the monumental human striving over the last four centuries, this gleaming, rippling intentionality; lift your hands from the heaving controls; leave the building. Calculation, purpose are nothing before this darkness. Give up. Sorrow is the one faint path. It isn't marked, not really a way at all.

*

What is the perfect life? asks Gregory of Nyssa. It is distinguished, he says, by unfixability, is a perpetual erotic craning. This is epektasis. He quotes St. Paul early in *The Life of Moses* — I strain toward the things that are to come. "Coming to a stop in the race was not safe for him. Why? Because no Good has its limit in its own nature but is limited by its opposite . . ." (i, 5). That is, for Gregory, by sin. When eros stops, ceases to be epektatic, it is because it has become something other than itself, its opposite in fact, which nevertheless is roughly camouflaged as eros. Being beguiled by the Good becomes one of the forms of rectitude. But their sharp symmetry betrays these counterfeits: "what is marked off by boundaries is not virtue" (i, 6).

Plato said that lack is constitutive of eros. The end of lack is the end of eros. Without absence and absence's opening out, there is something else, good intentions, piety, good management. It's like the people in the dialogues who shy away from the erotic business of philosophy because they fear to appear foolish or because they fear the "stripping" of the exercise. They devote themselves to what most people think of as philosophical activity — geometric speculation or otherworldly abstraction or butcher-like analysis or political theory or righteousness — but that is in fact a way to strangle the convulsive erotic energy of philosophy.

*

Asters and goldenrods are just starting to bloom in late July in the low hills above the river, but the flowers of middle summer are still here — coneflowers, bergamot, sunflowers, the clovers, wild flax. The grass is swollen, inebriated with an unconsidered muchness, prodigal; it seems to lift the light of my face into it, breathing this toward itself with an inhalation that begins its draw near my heels. The river now is a green stumble; it is thoughtless, magnificent, heavy. I've planted some wheat again this summer in the garden: entertainment, the community of the choir: the amorous pillar of the wheat altruistic, kenotic, bearing the weight of what can only be guessed at.

*

The life of virtue, says Gregory, the life of fundamental desire, has no border because this pursuit is participation in "nothing other than God". And "since this good has no limit, the participant's desire itself necessarily has no stopping place but stretches out with the limitless" (i, 7). You pass no threshold; there is no enlightenment, no final ecstasy, no restoration that feels as such of human consciousness to the world. "How then would one arrive at the sought-for boundary when he can find no boundary?"

The endlessness of desire is one of the poverties to which desire delivers you. One has no achievement, gain, to console, no stasis in which to found a home. But the homelessness of protean desire is the only human home, says Gregory: the restlessness, the self-sundering, the displacement — all this off-centredness, this reeling — is the one graceful movement.

Erotic poverty has no ambition, yet is alacritous: therefore no limit appears in the imagination it fosters for the essence of ambition is the idea of limitation. But such poverty must be given not chosen, otherwise it's a kind of opulence, a resplendence of the self and a diminution of the world. You may be roiled into it by desire. Better yet: fail into it and hold.

So: because what desire wants is unattainable, unreachable even by naming; because what it is is somehow participation in this unattainability, limitlessness, namelessness; because by its very nature it undermines what it erects, perpetuating itself by the finding of fresh absences, fundamental eros is epektatic. And because it is epektatic, it is impoverishing and because it is impoverishing, it may deliver you to the world. Or: because there is nothing near you, the world may gather closer.

> The soul, having gone out at the word of her Beloved, looks for Him, but does not find Him. She calls on him, though He can't be reached by any verbal symbol, and she is told by the watchman that she is in love with the unattainable, and that the object of her longing cannot be apprehended. In this way she is, in a certain sense, wounded and beaten because of the frustration of what she desires, now that she thinks that her yearning for the Other cannot be fulfilled or satisfied. But the veil of her grief is removed when she learns that the true satisfaction of her desire consists in constantly going on with her quest and never ceasing in her ascent, seeing that every fulfilment of her desire continually generates further desire for the Transcendent.

So says Gregory of Nyssa in his *Commentary on the Song of Songs* (xii: 1037). This is the vision of God: never to be satisfied in the desire to see him, he says in *The Life of Moses*.

What is crucial is the simultaneity of the unstinting press of desire and the unbroken frustration of the

imagination — the expectations, the certitudes, the
points of rest — that had grown around this desire as,
it seemed, its inevitable articulations. Erotic craning
and the failure of what seemed the essence of this
craning — all the language about it that apparently
uttered it. Desire goes on: what else is there to do?
Where else is there home but in the home-sundering
reach of desire?

*

Things go wrong; you are shrunk; you immediately
manoeuvre to recoup what has been lost. Desire's late,
scentless flower: loss. But what is better, says Simone
Weil, is to hold the pose of emptiness. Why? Because
this is the most erotic choice; it is the move with the
long breath in it, the future furled, the way that is least
like the self and can draw toward it otherness. But
how to stand in emptiness, to want as food the
tastelessness of having nothing? Place yourself
beneath irrational things, said the monks in the desert,
and know they are without blame.

There is the river, the shack, the tumbledown, scrub
land of the river. And, these days, the hills are thick-
faced with grass, bloom-plump. What if everything
were not better than you, what if the grass were not
better? Place yourself beneath irrational things. Go
under the government of the river; you go into the
school of the grass. Where else to learn the poverty
eros has taught you to want, where else to stand when
the project of self is set aside? Esteem having nothing
and watch how gracefully these other things hold this;
compete in staturelessness with things that do not
strive. The river, mindless, beams with an intelligence
beyond me, ridiculous to imagine I have any

advantage here. With luck, I'll slide under the phlox and speak. I'll go into the sandhills and dig a hole.

The endlessness of desire offers no clarity, no overview; it doesn't appear in analysis: it's just an ache, a wound, vulnus amoris, as Origen says in his commentary on the *Songs*. There is no consolation of judgement here, no calm of management. But there is conviction, sometimes stomach-turning: I must want the nothing that's all that's offered. And there is inebriation. Delight and praising.

*

A pewter light around the July river, the moult of its glide. And on the long grass banks, a quavering moth night. With things, as well, there is a cloud, the expanse of their unknowability. This distance, in one manifestation, is the effortless eccentricity of things, which is their generosity, what amasses the world. Things are far, unlike. This resistance to homogeneity in objects is what makes them a source of energy and also what makes the source of human loneliness. It's so impossible, too far: there's no returning to the world with grace: you will never enter the home of things. You have nowhere else to go but to be where you are and here you are inevitably homeless. Give up. I'd like to go to confession with the river. I'd like to be the novice of a deer.

*

God, says Gregory, is found in darkness. This is the darkness of the region beyond human powers: there the erotic soul goes "leaving behind everything that is observed, not only what sense comprehends, but also what the intelligence thinks it sees" and "it keeps on penetrating deeper until by intelligence's yearning for understanding it gains access to the invisible and the incomprehensible, and there it sees God" (*The Life of Moses,* ii, 163). But, he adds, while this is "the true knowledge of what is being sought," it is a "seeing that consists in not seeing". Intelligence's yearning brings it to the embarrassment of intelligence. To move this way toward the humiliation of intelligence, by the energy of intelligence, is, says Gregory, the way the soul is.

Looking involves an emigration from the look into a region of invisibility in the country of the thing. There is something other than the grass with the grass; this is the grass as distant, unassimilable, yet in its otherness beckoning. Beckoning but in flight from human seeing, understanding, concord. Beckoning but unreachable by what powers respond to the invitation. Eros goes on under the form of its own humiliation, under the guise of exhaustion, of giving up, bereft of any image of limit, empty of hope of satisfaction and nostalgic for this hope; it fails forward. It has gone and so it moves.

The seeing that is a not-seeing is a wooed obedience for Gregory, an apprehension which is a going from the self. Moses asks to see God face to face, but this, says Gregory, is a wildly impossible request: the only thing that can look absolute virtue in its face is evil for only "what is perceived to be opposite is face to face with the good" (ii, 254). So Moses is hidden in a hole in the rock and from that place espies the back of the passing Yahweh. But only one who follows can so apprehend. Virtue, contemplation and noesis become a single novel activity. Gregory's not seeing is a seeing which is not comprehension, but a decentring of the self in an unmeasured pursuit of what one desires, a headlongness which is virtue. A "seeing" which is a doing without calculation, a taking the life and movement of something else, something worthy of love.

I will go under the phlox and speak.

*

Caspian terns jive, hover and cut in the smudged luminosity above the late afternoon river, swaying in luxurious, violin-like turns a foot above the water. Their mastery is casual, a shrug, but always their moves are exact, utterly new things, shinings-forth from absence. The terns are catching moths just above the flow, dropping their tails for quick down-jags, flicking their heads to the side, short-stops' glove hands, no hitch in their flight, big bends just a few feet ahead. A music and a flowering forth. There is nothing more needed: anything else would be temptation, anything else would nudge this toward inconsequence. Human awe here is a stumbling mimesis, an awkward singing-along-with.

Each move in that small region just over the water could found a life, has the pitch of paradigm and is simply tossed off. Having no home, while bending into the world where one would live as if it were home, is the human home. The refusal of this paradox, its littling, is the source of any pursuit of firm control and the delimitation of the probe of desire. The experience of moving erotic homelessness is us in the world as the grass is the grass and the river is itself.

GLOSSARY

apokatastasis: In Plato and Cicero, the word is used
for the return of the stars to their initial position;
in a discussion of pleasure, Aristotle has it name
the restoration of a being to its first state. It was
also a medical term in the ancient world, referring
to the re-establishment of an original condition, as
in the re-setting of a joint.

In Origen, it designates both a therapy,
drawing an individual back to a condition of
nature, and the achievement of an accord —
amounting to an identity — among all things, a
"remembering" of a community beyond
imagination, yet within the scope of desire.

apophasis: The word is formed from "apo" — "from,
away from, asunder" — and "phasis" — "to
speak, report". "Mention of something we feign to
deny" *(Klein's Comprehensive Etymology)*. It is
address, in negative theology, appropriate to what
is beyond what the tongue can manage, an
asserting of names, a removing of names. It may
have the rhythm of praise.

ascesis: From the Greek for exercise, practice,
    training. It was used to describe the physical
    preparation of athletes. Ascesis has been
    understood usually as the will's schooling of the
    passions, but it also can be seen as the gathering
    and speeding of the self reformed by
    contemplation. Erotic reaching shapes — thins —
    the one who reaches. The self engined by
    contemplation, by the craning of eros, becomes a
    glyph for what can't be said but what draws
    desire.

epektasis: From ep-ek-teinomai, to reach out after.
    Fundamental desire is unsatisfiable, always in
    some measure empty, always ingenious. Epektasis
    is this unbroken reaching arising from eros'
    emptiness and ingenuity. The desire-filled
    stumbling of the erotic individual is part of the
    poverty out of which courtesy issues.

haecceitas: "This-ness": for John Duns Scotus, it was
    what made for the individuality of a thing, its
    singularity — a property such that exactly one
    individual could have it.

penthos: "Penthos is a sorrowful disposition of the
    soul, caused by the privation of something
    desirable" (Gregory of Nyssa). It is the state to
    which desire comes as it presses toward what
    language cannot circumscribe, divinity or
    wilderness. Penthos is not the extinction of eros
    but the form of its continuance.

"Mourning that may arise from the loss of relatives or friends; sadness over any mishap; lamentation for a dead god" (Irénée Hausherr, S.J., *Penthos, The Doctrine of Compunction in the Christian East*).

READING

Phaedrus, Plato
Symposium, Plato
Republic, Plato
The Lausiac History, Palladius
The Divine Names, pseudo-Dionysius the Areopagite
The Mystical Theology, pseudo-Dionysius the Areopagite
The Life of Moses, Gregory of Nyssa
Theological Orations, Gregory of Nazianzen
Periphyseon, John Scotus Eriugena
The Cloud of Unknowing, anonymous
Meditations on First Philosophy, René Descartes
Gravity and Grace, Simone Weil

NOTES
ON THE
Text

"How To Be Here?" and "There Is No Presence" were published previously in *Brick* magazine. "How To Be Here?" also appeared in the essay collection *Poetry and Knowing* (Quarry Press, 1995). "Contemplation and Cosmology" was first printed in *The Fiddlehead* (Winter, 1993).

Date